HIDDEN HISTORY
of
VICKSBURG

Ryan Starrett and Josh Foreman

THE
History
PRESS

Published by The History Press
Charleston, SC
www.historypress.com

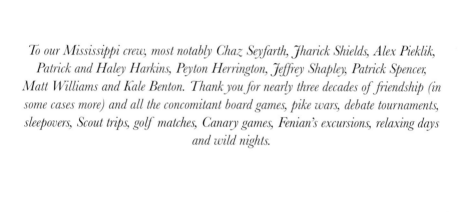

To our Mississippi crew, most notably Chaz Seyfarth, Jharick Shields, Alex Pieklik, Patrick and Haley Harkins, Peyton Herrington, Jeffrey Shapley, Patrick Spencer, Matt Williams and Kale Benton. Thank you for nearly three decades of friendship (in some cases more) and all the concomitant board games, pike wars, debate tournaments, sleepovers, Scout trips, golf matches, Canary games, Fenian's excursions, relaxing days and wild nights.

CONTENTS

1. Fort St. Pierre: Where the Mississippi
   and Yazoo Rivers Meet 7

2. Judge Lynch Comes to Vicksburg: A Rough Young Town
   Rages Against the Gamblers......................................21

3. The Local Incel: Vicksburg Through the Eyes of the Lonely,
   Lustful and Literary Edwin A. 31

4. The Siege of Vicksburg: General John Bowen Meets
   a Soldier's Death 42

5. The *Sultana*: America's Deadliest Boat................................52

6. A Wife, a War; Another Wife, Another War: Jefferson Davis
   and Brierfield Plantation 64

7. Sister Mary Ignatius Sumner and the Sisters of Mercy.......................78

8. Ricochet: Act Like a Man, Die Like a Fool 94

9. Joseph Biedenharn and the Bottling of Coca-Cola...........................104

10. A Walker in Vicksburg 113

11. The Bad Man: Rafael McCloud and Vicksburg's
     Week of Fear 124

12. The Oak: "Across the River and Under the
     Shade of the Tree" 132

Notes 143
Selected Bibliography...157
About the Authors 160

FORT ST. PIERRE

Where the Mississippi and Yazoo Rivers Meet

THE LAST DAYS OF JULY 1702

Father Nicholas Foucault was looking forward to a rest. He had been working among the Arkansas Natives for a year and was frustrated and depressed. He had made little progress among the Natives, and when two French soldiers entered his village to settle a dispute between the Illinois and Chickasaw, Foucault decided to accompany them back to Mobile when their mission was completed.

While among the Arkansas, the soldiers grew sick, and Foucault decided to hire four visiting Koroa Natives to paddle him and the Frenchmen down the Mississippi River to the Yazoo River. When they reached the village of the Yazoo, the priest paid his guides and began to set up his altar for Mass.

But Father Foucault would never finish that final Mass.

Father Antoine Davion was traveling north to visit the French mission among the Arkansas. When he reached the Yazoo and Mississippi Rivers, he was horrified to find the still-erected altar abandoned. Father Foucault and his companions were gone. But Father Davion recognized the hat of his friend, some of the equipment he used for Mass and a handful of his papers strewn about the ground.[1]

Father Davion fled back to the safety of Mobile, fled this strange bluff between two rivers, fled from the fertile land between the Father of Waters and the River of Death that had now, for the first time, absorbed the blood of Europeans to mix with the blood of those who came before—and

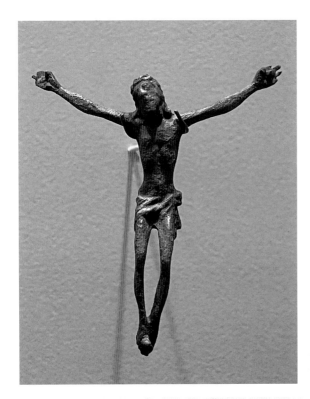

Left: Crucifix found at Fort St. Pierre, housed at the Museum of Mississippi History. *Ryan Starrett.*

Below: A 1911 print of Jacques Marquette and Louis Joliet in a canoe in 1673. *Library of Congress.*

those who came first—and prepared to mingle with the blood of tens of thousands more in a city that one day would be synonymous with suffering and death: Vicksburg.

The French were determined to build an empire. Their rivals, Spain and Britain, had solidified themselves to the south and east. The French possessed enormous amounts of land but lacked the instant wealth provided by the silver and gold of Spanish lands and the human capital of the British. As a result, French policy hinged on trade, which required good relations with the Natives. So, posts, or concessions, were established west along the St. Lawrence River in Canada and then south along the Ohio and Mississippi Rivers. At the same time the French were pushing south through Illinois Territory, another contingent had settled along the Gulf Coast and began moving up the Mississippi River, both forces establishing posts along the way and pushing the two frontiers closer and closer, hoping to control the north, south and interior of a continent.

Fort St. Pierre

1719

In 1699, the French established a beachhead in Biloxi.[2] Seventeen years later, they settled their most profitable concession in Natchez, atop a bluff, along the Mississippi River. Three years later, they pushed their boundary eighty miles north to the banks of the Yazoo River. The ever-gallivanting chronicler and adventurer Andre Penicaut wrote:

> *M. de Bienville sent M. de la Boulaye, a lieutenant, with thirty men and a great deal of munitions and merchandise to establish a fort close to the village of the Yasoux. When he got there, he chose the highest place he could find on the bank of the river, on the right side four leagues inland from its mouth, two musket shots from their village, and there he had his fort built.[3]*

Model of Fort St. Pierre at the Museum of Mississippi History. *Ryan Starrett.*

Fort St. Pierre was a square wooden palisade surrounded by a moat six feet across and three feet deep.[4] Four bastions fitted with swivel guns protected each corner. A ramp crossed the moat in the direction of the Yazoo River, allowing access to the fertile fields beyond where farmers worked and plantations were cleared. Inside the fort stood a warehouse, barracks for the soldiers and commandant, a Roman Catholic church and a house for the interpreter who would play an indispensable role between the settlers and the Natives. The most unique structure—which demonstrated the military importance (as well as danger and fickleness of the times)—was the shot tower, where soldiers could climb to the top and dump molten lead through a sieve. As the rounded projectiles fell, they were shaped into musket balls before they plunged into a container of water at the tower's base.

The fort and its surrounding community were expected to become self-sufficient. There would be little traffic in the way of supplies going up the Mississippi River and down the Yazoo River. Yet the land was so lush, and newly arriving colonists so eager to settle on their piece of paradise, that the supply issue initially posed little impediment.

Hundreds flocked to Fort St. Pierre and its environs. In 1719, 82 French persons settled along the Yazoo. Within one year, another 308 joined them, including M. le Blanc, the French minister of war, who wasted little time in clearing a massive plantation, which included not only the main house but also an additional ten houses for the 60 workers he employed, a garden, a house for the gardener, a separate house for the interpreter he planned to utilize, a reservoir and a baking oven.[5]

The concession along the Yazoo River was off to an auspicious start. When Diron D'Artaguiette visited the area in 1723, he reported, "It is at this fort where I have seen the best disciplined troops and where the duty is performed with exactitude, thanks to the attention of the commandant."[6] Fort St. Pierre was, indeed, an intimidating structure designed to both facilitate trade with the local Natives and protect French persons and interests along the Yazoo River.

Unfortunately for the settlers, the fort and its garrison were in excellent condition for a good reason: the survival of the community depended on its presence.

Just one year before D'Artaguitte's glowing report, a murder sent a reminder to the colonists around Fort St. Pierre: they were living on borrowed land.

French and Native wax models at the Museum of Mississippi History. *Ryan Starrett.*

1722

Two sergeants, Riter and Desnoyers, eager to significantly add to their meager soldier's pay, acquired two tracts of land and began to improve the land. They each built a cabin in which they resided when not on duty. Being soldiers, they were entitled to spend each night in the fort but preferred their newly erected cabins.

Sergeant Riter was so pleased with his land and so confident in his ability to tame it that he brought his wife and teenaged son to stay with him. He was not so naive as to neglect to bring a small arsenal consisting of seven or eight guns, most of which he kept loaded and within reach at all times. Those firearms might have saved his life had they *all* been loaded.

One dark night, a Chickasaw raiding party crept up to Riter's unfinished cabin and entered through the curtained door. Riter fired the first weapon he grabbed, but it was unloaded. The Chickasaws were upon him with tomahawk and scalping knife. Riter's wife was dragged to a nearby ravine, as either a new slave of the Chickasaws or to be sold elsewhere. Her fate was neither. Attempting to escape, she attacked her kidnappers with a hidden knife and was quickly shot down with arrows, her body falling into the ravine. Frightened, their young son bolted from the cabin and ran toward the fort, screaming. A fast-thinking warrior was immediately upon him; he scalped his head and slit his throat. Neither slash was fatal, but the boy was left for dead.

A woken Sergeant Desnoyers fired his gun in the air, alerting the fort. Soldiers emerged, and the warriors fled. The pursuing force located the bodies of the three French settlers. Sergeant Riter and his son, still alive, were carried back to Fort St. Pierre, where the former perished less than three weeks later. Sergeant Riter's wife never made it back to the fort that had been built to protect her.[7]

When D'Artaguiette visited Fort St. Pierre the next year, the fort was in good condition and its garrison vigilant. Shortly thereafter, the residents lost interest in the region. Most left, many to Natchez. Fort St. Pierre fell into disrepair. Its garrison dwindled; its defenses relaxed.

From *Histoire de la Louisiane*, vol. 2, by Antoine Simone Le Page du Pratz (1758): *top, left*: a Natchez man; *top, right*: a Natchez woman; *bottom*: scenes of torture. *New York Public Library*.

✍

November 1729

Sieur de Coder, the commandant of Fort St. Pierre, decided it was time to head south. Business, information and gossip were booming at Fort Rosalie. The Yazoo concession was stable but shrinking. Fort Rosalie was a different story. And then there were old comrades to visit. Sergeant Desnoyers, who had fired the shot seven years prior that had sent the Chickasaw scrambling and saved his friend, Sergeant Riter's son—not to mention Fort St. Pierre itself—was now running the speculator M. le Blanc's concession in Natchez. Desnoyer had done well for himself, rising to second lieutenant and director of one of Natchez's most profitable concessions. In rank, he was just under the commandant, Sieur de Chepart.

Sieur de Coder combed his long, thick locks prior to the journey, stepped outside his house inside Fort St. Pierre and met his escort, along with Le Hou, the storekeeper. The company proceeded to the land of the Natchez and Fort Rosalie.

✍

NATCHEZ

November 28, 1729

The Natchez marched slowly and in unison toward Fort Rosalie. The great chief and his warriors carried the calumet to smoke with the French chief. They brought gifts as well.

The drums beat, the march continued, slowly, formally, in rhythm, past Ricard, Rosalie's storekeeper—who had gone to the river to take care of business—and toward the fort. French residents drifted toward the fort to see both the dance of the Natchez and the gifts they brought. St. Pierre's Commandant Coder and its old resident Desnoyer watched as the gifts were laid on the ground and the Natchez began to disperse around the compound.

And then the massacre at the fort commenced. Just as quickly, it was over. Just like that.

Rosalie's Commandant Chepart, Pierre's Commandant Coder, the soldier turned overseer Desnoyer and everyone else but one in Fort Rosalie was dead or mortally wounded within minutes. Sieur du Coder received special postmortem treatment on account of his long, scalp-worthy hair.[8]

Those killed so quickly in the fort were the fortunate ones.

St. Pierre's storekeeper, Le Hou, fended off the initial attack and, though wounded, escaped into the woods. Three or four days later, his wounds getting the better of him, he began to cry out for assistance.

One of the two male captives taken by the Natchez, Lebeau—the tailor condemned to alter the clothes of his dead countrymen into garments fitted for his captors—was sent into the woods with a promise that the supplicant would be spared if he returned to the village. Le Hou acquiesced. Shortly after, his headless corpse slumped to the ground.[9]

Lebeau, the tailor, was forced to the riverfront again. He had been busy turning his acquaintances' and friends' clothes into garments for their killers. Now, for the second time, he was summoned to the river to beckon another pirogue of his countrymen to the shore. Terrified of the consequences should he refuse, he again performed the odious task.

This time, three of the five French voyageurs mercifully died in the first fusillade. One escaped, but the fifth, Gratien, fell into Natchez hands.

His tormenters made him run to the village while they pressed their muskets into his skin and fired burning black powder blanks into his flesh along the

The Natchez Massacre, by John J. Egan (1850). *Saint Louis Art Museum.*

way. Upon arrival, he was sentenced to death and sent to the temple, where two perpendicular and two horizontal poles had been constructed. He was tied to the poles in an X shape while his tormentors built bundles of cane into a fire. As he awaited death, Gratien noticed a group of Frenchwomen nearby and called out to them. He identified himself by name and told them that he was a worker at Fort St. Pierre, and he begged them to pray for him. Then the Natchez approached and began to place the lighted canes all over his body, burning him slowly to death.[10]

The massacre at Fort Rosalie and the executions in the following days claimed the lives of 235 French men, women and children. Another 230 were taken into captivity, many of whom would be executed in the coming months.[11]

For four weeks, life went on as usual at Fort St. Pierre.

One of the few to escape the massacre at Fort Rosalie was the fort's storekeeper, Sieur Ricard. He had been down at the river when the attack commenced. He proceeded to swim to the other shore and hide in a forest until dark. Not wanting to risk wandering along the shore, Ricard stepped into the river up to his neck and walked about three and a half miles to the cabin of a nearby settler. Ricard saw a light on and entered the cabin, only

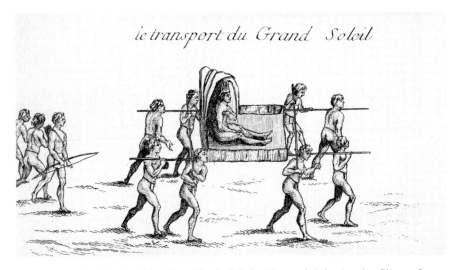

Transporting the Natchez chief, from *Histoire de la Louisiane*, vol. 2, by Antoine Simone Le Page du Pratz (1758). *New York Public Library.*

to find a detachment of Natives eating inside. While he was terrified, Ricard was told to enter, sit down and eat. To his great relief, the band belonged to the friendly Yazoo from the vicinity of Fort St. Pierre. The Yazoo gave the grateful Frenchman a pirogue, in which he made his escape.[12]

Ricard had no way of knowing that the very warriors who had saved him had arrived in Natchez just days prior to smoke the calumet[13] with the Natchez. The latter, not wishing to reveal their bloody intentions, asked the Yazoo to wait. In the interval, Ricard made his escape. When his benefactors stood before Natchez's great chief three days later at the calumet ceremony, with Fort Rosalie and French houses smoldering in the background, they were told that the Choctaws had already eliminated the French in New Orleans. The Yazoo agreed to eradicate the last remaining Frenchmen at Fort St. Pierre.

❧

ST. PIERRE

December 31, 1729

The Jesuit priest John Souel was making his way back to his house after a visit with the chief of the Yazoo. He lived about three miles from Fort St. Pierre. As he crossed a ravine, musket fire erupted, and the priest sank to the earth, dead. The Yazoo stripped him of his cassock and proceeded to his house, where they killed his servant and plundered his possessions.[14]

With commandant Sieur de Coder killed at Fort Rosalie and the rest of the concession's inhabitants dwindling over the previous seven years, only twenty Frenchmen remained at Fort St. Pierre when the Yazoo arrived. News of the massacre at Natchez had not yet reached the northern fort. (Those who survived fled south to New Orleans.) As the friendly Yazoo entered the fort in large numbers and began milling aimlessly among the cabins, the inhabitants suspected nothing. The fort had an open-door policy and had been established to trade with these very Yazoo.[15] No one suspected anything until the first tomahawks and war clubs came crashing down.

The surprise was complete. Within minutes, all the inhabitants of Fort St. Pierre were dead, with the exception of nine women and children who were taken as captives.[16]

January 1, 1730

Father Stephen Doutreleau and four French voyageurs disembarked at the base of the Yazoo River. Though he was close to his destination, the home of his friend and fellow Jesuit Father Souel, Doutreleau knew he would not arrive in time for Mass. So, he set up his altar and prepared to celebrate the sacred rites.

As he finished his preparations, a band of Yazoo paddled up, expressing friendship. The French and Yazoo mingled as the priest completed his preparations. Just before Mass began, the voyageurs fired their muskets at some passing buzzards. They did not reload but instead turned their attention to the Mass, which had begun. The Yazoo, too, feigned piety as they placed themselves behind the Frenchmen. As the priest began to chant the *Kyrie*, the Yazoo unloaded their own muskets, killing one voyageur and striking another in the leg and Father Doutreleau in the arm. The living voyageurs darted to their boats as the Yazoo fired another round at the priest. They missed, and Father Doutreleau likewise fled to the boat. As the four pushed off, a ball struck Doutreleau in the mouth and lodged in his gums. But he had reached the boat, and after an hour-long chase, the Yazoo called off the pursuit.

The four frightened companions planned to report the attack to the authorities at Fort Rosalie. As they approached the settlement, Natchez Natives stood at the bank, waving in a friendly manner and offering refuge. When the weary and fleeing French saw the burned fort and houses, they wisely declined the Natchez hospitality and continued to what they hoped was safety in New Orleans.[17]

January 1730–March 1730

French retaliation was inevitable, and an alliance of French, Choctaw and Tunica was quickly assembled. One month after the massacre at Fort St. Pierre and two months after the attack at Fort Rosalie, the Choctaw, acting alone, freed fifty-one captives.[18] One month later, the French and Tunicas, having finally joined up with the Choctaws, secured the remainder of the

Depiction of a Native from Northwest Louisiana (1741). *New York Public Library*.

"Equipage des Chasseurs Sauvages Canadiens," early 1700s. *Beinecke Library at Yale University.*

captives. As a final parting shot, the Natchez released the survivors not to the French but to the Choctaw, who, in turn, held the women and children until the French paid a large ransom. The last of the survivors, after two months of harrowing captivity, stumbled into New Orleans, where they were loaned sixty livres for clothes and necessities to begin their new life.[19]

Meanwhile, the societies of the Natchez and Yazoo, destroyers of two French forts and more than 250 French persons, was on the wane. The French, Choctaw and Tunica were about to enact a more thorough and permanent extermination of the Natchez and Yazoo than the French had suffered at Forts Rosalie and St. Pierre.

JUDGE LYNCH COMES TO VICKSBURG

A Rough Young Town Rages Against the Gamblers

THE BARBECUE

The Fourth of July barbecue—it was the greatest of American celebrations. Roasted animals, military parades, toasts, speeches, drinking and dancing. The tradition had developed and spread across the South in the decades since the War for American Independence. By 1835, it had been honed to a well-orchestrated spectacle.

A month before Independence Day 1835, Vicksburg's volunteer militia met to form a "committee of arrangements." The volunteers would make sure Vicksburg enjoyed its own extravagant Fourth of July celebration. It would be held at Springfield, a neighborhood on the border of the city. Space would be required for the celebration, and the entire town—the entire county—would be invited.

By the early decades of the nineteenth century, Fourth of July barbecues had become "formal and standardized" across the American South. Historian Robert F. Moss wrote, "Town after town celebrated the Fourth with an almost identical set of ceremonies that featured barbecue at their center." Though we know much more about the details of what happened *after* the Vicksburg Fourth of July celebration than what occurred before or during it, we can use John James Audubon's description of another Fourth of July barbecue, held around the same time in Kentucky, to imagine Vicksburg's.

Brush would have been cleared, tree limbs trimmed and a carpet of grass prepared for the partygoers. Tables would have been placed in the clearing.

The trees would provide some shade from the burning July sun. Animals would have been procured—pigs, cows, deer, turkeys, chickens, sheep and maybe even a squirrel or two. Some of the animals may have even been led to the festival grounds and slaughtered there. Summer fruits—peaches, plums and pears—would have been collected and drinks of all kinds transported there. In Vicksburg, that meant American brandy, European wine, whiskey—some fine, some swill—and cider. A nearby spring would have supplied fresh water.

On the day of the event, attendees would have formed a column behind the Volunteers, dressed in uniform, who would then have marched to the barbecue site. At the site, the Declaration of Independence would have been read, patriotic songs sung and a lecture delivered by an orator, usually a prominent member of society. In Vicksburg, the committee chose the lawyer and amateur historian John M. Chilton. William H. Benton, a lawyer, postmaster and former mayor of Vicksburg, would read the Declaration of Independence. After the barbecue, the Volunteers would drill in the city square.

To cook the feast, a four-to-six-foot-wide trench would have been dug that could have been dozens of feet long, depending on how much meat had to be cooked. Hardwood would have been loaded into the trench and

The traditional method of making "pit" barbecue, photographed at the Atlanta Exposition in 1896. *New York Public Library.*

burned to coals. Animals—either whole or cut in half lengthways—would then have been spitted and laid over the trench. Multiple cooks would have tended to the meat, basting it with butter, vinegar, water, salt and pepper and then turning the meat over when necessary. Enslaved people likely would have done much of the cooking and tending, as plantation cooking fell largely to them. They might have even added African flavors to the meat: garlic and red pepper. They also might have added herbs, such as coriander, sage and basil.[20]

During the feast, partygoers would have toasted thirteen times—to the Fourth of July, to the signers of the Declaration, to the soldiers of the Revolution, to General Washington, to Mississippi, to women, and so on. Drinks would have been flowing on that Fourth of July 1835, and spirits would have been high.

But we know for sure that tension was growing. A newspaper advertisement for the barbecue had claimed: "the citizens of Vicksburg and its vicinity are invited to attend." But not all people were welcome. A professional gambler, Francis Cabler, had shown up. He had worked his way to the table where the toasts were being given. And he was making an ass of himself.[21]

When Cabler was asked by an officer of the Vicksburg Volunteers to quiet down, he insulted the officer. When a partygoer tried to intervene, Cabler began beating him. The whole of the celebration then turned on Cabler, forcibly expelling him from the barbecue.

The celebration resumed, but it was now suffused with a sense of foreboding. The Volunteers prepared to march to the square. There, Cabler resurfaced with an entourage. His face must have betrayed his "nefarious design"— two Volunteers grabbed and restrained him immediately. They found on his person a loaded pistol, a large knife (the Bowie knife was popular then) and a dagger. The Volunteers, along with a crowd of Vicksburg citizens, marched Cabler to the woods. They tied him to a tree, whipped him and tarred and feathered him. They told him to leave Vicksburg within forty-eight hours.[22]

Cabler's friends must have been conspicuously irate. As an eyewitness account published in the *Vicksburg Register* put it, "In the meantime, one of his comrades, the Lucifer of the gang, had been endeavoring to rally and arm his confederates for the purpose of rescuing him—which, however, he failed to accomplish."[23]

Fearful that they had "aggravated the whole band of these desperadoes and feeling no security against their vengeance," a large group of Vicksburg citizens met that night to draft a resolution: all professional gamblers were required to leave Vicksburg within twenty-four hours.

The resolution was printed on a handbill the next morning and posted at street corners in Vicksburg.

Many of the town's professional gamblers fled—but not all. The citizens of Vicksburg had hoped to avoid a "bloody termination" to the events that had begun on the Fourth—at least according to a newspaper report. But the next day, Vicksburg would get its bloody termination six times over. And the story would spread to every corner of the country. Vicksburg would become synonymous with mob violence.

CITY OF STRANGERS

The Vicksburg of the 1830s was young, unpolished and brutal, but it was also bustling, attractive and aspirational. The city had been founded only in 1819. At the time of its founding, from the farmlands of a methodist minister, it was "practically nothing," as one historian put it, not even noticeable from the river. But its high bluffs and position on the Mississippi River, near where the Yazoo River merged with it, made it a natural focal point for settlers. It grew to have more than 2,000 residents by the early 1830s. As Choctaw cessions opened up land for cotton farming in the Mississippi interior, planters looked to Vicksburg as the port from which they could access the Mississippi River and New Orleans. Soon, Vicksburg rivaled Natchez as the premier commercial center of the state. Between 1830 and 1840, the population of Warren County grew from 7,861 to 15,820. By the mid-1830s, more than forty thousand bales of cotton were leaving Vicksburg's port each year.[24]

Vicksburg was a city alive with doctors, lawyers, businessmen and bankers, a middle class of professionals who found customers in the commercial city. Farmers from the region cut ruts in Vicksburg's muddy streets, bringing their produce to market and to the river. Stagecoaches and a horse-drawn rail connected the city to Clinton, Jackson and Yazoo City. In addition to being a destination for cotton, Vicksburg also had "an exploding slave market," as another historian put it. The number of enslaved people in Warren County more than doubled from 4,483 in 1830 to 10,493 in 1840. Enslaved people outnumbered white people 2 to 1. The presence of the slave trade added an element of repressive paranoia to Vicksburg society, with white residents ever wary of a slave revolt. The Vicksburg Volunteers patrolled the city at night, checking the passes of any Black people they encountered.[25]

Mississippi river gamblers, from *Forty Years a Gambler on the Mississippi*, by George Devol (1894). *Library of Congress.*

The city had grown so quickly that its buildings felt slapdash. Its wooden structures were unpainted, and customers perused shops along wooden walkways—walkways that kept them out of muddy, trash-strewn streets. Rain washed gullies and ravines into the city's hillsides. Visitors' accommodations were filthy.[26]

The river connected the city to places far beyond. Historian Pamela Lea Grillis described the impact that the river—and the people who worked it—had on daily life in Vicksburg:

> *On any given day, more than 400 boats might be docked at the riverfront. Each one of those had at least four to five crew members. After braving a perilous journey up or down the treacherous Mississippi, these men recognized no one's authority over them.*

They felt more at home in Vicksburg, Grillis wrote, than in any other river port. Vicksburg's status as a young and plucky town with a "large, professional middle class" and an "independent-spirited working class" was inviting to the riverboat men. There was no aristocracy to dictate strictures of behavior. It was a "wild and rambunctious town." But it was aiming to civilize, with the establishment of churches, religious societies, schools, a hospital, a theater and a Masonic lodge. And its middle class was aspiring to respectability.[27]

Vicksburg's sudden ascendancy to a position of economic importance on the river meant that there was a lot of money to be made there. People came to Vicksburg from all over. No one who lived in Vicksburg had been there for very long. As historian Joshua Rothman put it, they were "itinerants who lacked strong ties to each other or to any given community....Vicksburg was a place people tended to pass through rather than remain."[28]

The one thing the riverboat men, slave traders, planters, middle-class professionals and full-time gamblers had in common was their fanatical desire to get rich—and to do it quickly. "Most people in Vicksburg were essentially speculators who had risked migration to the Southwest for the allure of fast profits almost unimaginable anywhere else in the country," Rothman wrote. "In a very real sense, nearly everyone in Vicksburg was a gambler."

They were gamblers in a figurative sense but also in a literal sense. One former professional gambler, writing at the time, estimated that three-quarters of Vicksburg was "more or less addicted to gambling." The popular games of chance at the time were roulette, cards and faro. The professional gamblers would make their money at these games, preying on the ignorant and cheating when opportune. For many citizens of Vicksburg, these professionals, who seemed to be accumulating in the city, were too much to tolerate. They were too brazen, too loud, too violent, too drunk, too unscrupulous—and had created too much ill will with community members who had lost money to them. In the words of one newspaper account, "It appears that some persons had kept a gambling house in Vicksburg for some time, and, as usual in similar establishments, had their pimps and their decoys employed, inveigling inexperienced young men into the lion's den, where they were inevitably fleeced of all they possessed, and frequently ill-treated by the conductors."[29]

On Monday, July 6, the Vicksburg Volunteers led a mob of hundreds of Vicksburg citizens to the area where the professional gamblers operated. They went from gambling house to gambling house, pulling out faro tables and other gambling paraphernalia, checking for straggling gamblers. When they got to Truman North's coffeehouse (*coffeehouse* was often code for *gambling den*), the mob learned that a group of gamblers had barricaded themselves

People Playing Cards at an Inn, by Jan Ekels II (1784). *Rijksmuseum.*

inside. The mob surrounded the house and waited for the men to surrender. When they didn't, the Volunteers kicked in the back door.

Immediately, the men inside opened fire. Dr. Hugh Bodley, a twenty-eight-year-old physician from a powerful Kentucky family, was hit and killed. When Bodley fell, the mob became enraged, shooting into the house and forcing their way into every door. They dragged out four men, one of whom had been shot but was still alive. North, whom the mob considered the "ringleader" of the plot to defy the citizens' order to leave Vicksburg, was not inside the building. But he was captured soon after as he was trying to flee the city.

The mob marched the five men, identified in a newspaper account later as "North, Hullams, Dutch Bill, Smith, and McCall," to the gallows in the public square "in silence." They were hanged immediately. Their bodies were left dangling for a day before they were cut down and buried in a ditch.

SHAPING THE NARRATIVE

The eyewitness account that appeared in newspapers following the execution was published by William Mills, the editor of the *Vicksburg Register*. Mills spun the summary execution of the five men as the justifiable—and even "necessary"—actions of Vicksburg's upright citizens. "We are proud of the public spirit and indignation against offenders displayed by the citizens, and congratulate them on having at length banished a class of individuals whose shameless vices and daring outrages have long poisoned the springs of morality, and interrupted the relations of society."

Mills knew that the mob's actions would draw scrutiny, writing, "It is not expected that this act will pass without censure from those who had not an opportunity of knowing and feeling the dire necessity out of which it originated." Again, he stressed the necessity of the mob's actions: "We had borne with their enormities, until to have suffered them any longer would not only have proved us to be destitute of every manly sentiment, but would also have implicated us in the guilt of accessories to their crimes." In other words, things had gotten so bad in Vicksburg that the summary execution of the five men was absolutely necessary. Actually, *not* executing the men would have been the real crime. Anyone who disagreed just didn't understand Vicksburg.[30]

Mills's effort to spin the violence as a virtuous act was not successful. As Rothman wrote, "The Vicksburg rioters found few supporters outside the city. Instead, across the nation 'Vicksburg' became a byword for unjustifiable violence and the excesses of mob rule that threatened to undermine the authority of the law, if not republican government itself."[31]

Police in Warren County did their part to reinforce the assertion that the killings were necessary. At a meeting of Warren County citizens the day after the executions, the president of the board of police read the following resolution: "Resolved, also, that the summary justice inflicted on the murderers of our late estimable citizen, Doctor Hugh S. Bodley, was justifiable; and that the citizens of the county do and will sustain the citizens of the town, in that execution of speedy and retributive justice." The resolution was adopted unanimously.[32]

When Mills's account spread around the country, some questioned the veracity of his narrative. Hezekiah Niles, who published a national magazine in Baltimore called the *Weekly Register*, questioned the "specious character" of the narrative. He said the executions at Vicksburg were "disgraceful to all concerned." "Of all the harpies which prey upon the public, the professed

A depiction of the lynching of the Vicksburg gamblers, from the *American Anti-Slavery Almanac* (1894). *New York Public Library.*

gambler is the most offensive in our eyes," Niles wrote. "But we would not exterminate him at such a fearful sacrifice as the people of Vicksburg have made on the shrine of passion."[33]

Duke W. Hullum, the father of one of the men executed at Vicksburg, wrote an open letter to the governor of Mississippi, complaining that authorities had not done anything to punish the vigilantes.[34]

Another eyewitness account was published in the New Orleans–based *Louisiana Advertiser* that painted a messier and bloodier picture of the executions. In the *Advertiser*'s account, the mob of hundreds who had rooted out the gamblers was actually composed of only a few dozen. Rather than leading the men silently to the gallows, the vigilantes tied ropes around their necks and dragged them to the public square. The gamblers begged for their lives, and the injured gambler was hanged before he even regained consciousness. A band played music while the act was carried out. Any Vicksburg citizens who tried to intervene were threatened with death by the mob. All the money found on the persons of the gamblers was piled on a table in front of their dangling bodies, and a committee distributed it to anyone who could prove they had lost money gambling with the men.[35]

Many outside Warren County, however, considered the executions to be outrageous violations of the law. One critic of the violence was no less than Abraham Lincoln, then only a lawyer. Lincoln's address to the Young Men's Lyceum in Springfield in 1838 focused on the dangers of "the increasing disregard for law which pervades the country…the worse than savage mobs for the executive ministers of justice." Lincoln saw mob violence as an existential threat to the United States. He called the execution of the Vicksburg gamblers "perhaps the most dangerous in example and revolting to humanity." Mob violence would punish the guilty, the innocent and even the perpetrators of the violence eventually. "Thus it goes on, step by step, till all the walls erected for the defense of the persons and property of individuals are trodden down and disregarded," he said. To him, the events in Vicksburg had weakened the foundation of American government.[36]

Lincoln asserted that the mob would inevitably turn on itself. Some in Vicksburg had tried to stop the hangings—and had been threatened with death themselves.

The leaders of the Vicksburg vigilantism had wanted to have their cornbread and eat it, too. They had wanted to skip the slow and tedious process of an arrest and trial and go straight to justice. But what they had actually accomplished was to join—and even trump—the professional gamblers' moral depravity.

3

The Local Incel

Vicksburg Through the Eyes of the Lonely, Lustful and Literary Edwin A.

In 1844, a Vicksburg resident identified only as "Edwin A." wrote a retrospective book, *A Walk through Vicksburgh*, about his two-year stay in the town. Throughout the book, he gives many details about life in early Vicksburg. He reliably expresses derision and confoundment toward the city. He seems to resent that Vicksburg citizens liked to have a good time—throwing balls and barbecues, going to the theater, betting on horses, flirting, fighting and drinking. He was revolted by the slave society Vicksburg was a part of and by the Southern chivalric traditions that required men to defend their honor by dueling.

But throughout the book, a central theme emerges: Edwin A. is obsessed with women. And they are repulsed by him.[37]

WHO WAS EDWIN A.?

He considered himself a "generous and intelligent mechanic" (to be a mechanic in the early 1800s was to be "bred to manual labor") and a "natural gentleman."[38] He was a self-described honest man who bore "that seal of reprobation—poverty!"[39] He never says exactly where he is from but references New York, New Jersey, Pennsylvania and New England and being "down east" generally.

The Young Mechanic, by Miner Kilbourne Kellogg (1800s). *Smithsonian American Art Museum.*

He references his "whiskers," which made him look like a bear. This suggests he wore a full beard, which was a somewhat unpopular style. According to a study of facial hair from the time, only around 10 percent of men wore a full beard in the early 1840s, whereas around 45 percent of men wore grown-out sideburns with a shaven chin and upper lip.[40]

Listings of men's clothing for sale in Vicksburg in 1844 gives us a clue about what he might have worn. Linen was popular and came in plaid, checked, striped, printed, earthtone and natural styles. Printed linen was reserved for short coats ("coatees"). Pantaloons were made of a ribbed linen. Cotton was a popular fabric as well, though the sellers had more linen options than cotton ones. Gloves and cravats were offered in different styles. Hats came in an assortment of styles: Russian beaver, Russian silk, Canadian straw, seagrass, Scottish, fur, glazed. Boots and "brogans"—a kind of heavy work shoe—were offered. Since Edwin A. referred to himself as impoverished, we can assume he was not wearing the finest articles Vicksburg merchants had to offer.[41]

Throughout the book, he expresses a deep and persistent sadness regarding his inability to find a female companion. In the preface, he explains that the whole reason he wrote the book was to "banish that insupportable prurience of an unsophisticated heart—caused by the absence of female society."

In a thirteen-stanza poem titled "The Poet to His Future Wife," Edwin A. imagines his wife, "which God's own hand hath made for me." She is kind, modest, prayerful, sensible, loving and meek; has a sweet voice; and will be a "help-mate through this weary life."

> *Then sweetly down the vale of time*
> *In unison of hearts we'll glide,*
> *And when our vigorous frames decline,*
> *We'll sweetly sleep by other's side.*
> *United both in soul and heart,*
> *That death divided—could not part."*

Sadly, the perfect wife Edwin A. wrote about is only imagined. As sweet as his vision of a wife is, his poem is laden with regret and frustration:

> *For disappointment follows me,*
> *And youth's bright hours uncheered pass,*
> *I now, alas, to fate's decree!*
> *And seek in vain for happiness.*
> *But hope relumes the mystic bourne,*
> *And bids my sad heart cease to mourn.*[42]

He had given up on courting after "trying for days and nights to make a breach in some hard heart; to catch the coquet eye that smiles on all alike within her reach." He was waiting for "some kindred heart" to "fall in love with me." In other words, he had begun to take a passive role in his search for a companion.[43]

In a short essay on the "fatal melancholy" that afflicts some people, Edwin A. gives a clue about his possible mental state: "To a person of exquisite sensibility, compelled by poverty to herd with those from whom they shrink as from a viper, and unable to select their own society, life hath no charms." He explained that as he composed his poem about Vicksburg, his heart turned toward the "dark side," and his poem began to ridicule the people of Vicksburg that he deemed "pretenders," "hypocrites," false gentlemen and prideful ladies. But he swore that "malice or revenge does not dwell in my bosom."

So, a vague picture of Edwin A. emerges: he was a bearded man who earned his living with his hands. Nevertheless, he was educated and literary. He shielded his face with a straw hat and wore breathable linen clothes. He was wary of losing a brogan in the sucking Vicksburg mud. And he skulked about Vicksburg, observing everything and everyone with a keen reporter's eye. His fellow citizens may or may not have known he was lonely, jaded and depressed.

"The Antipodes of Theirs."

Again and again, Edwin A. wrote about women—about their appearance, their behavior and the way they ought to look and behave. And he documented the slights and mistreatment that women directed his way. They literally would not give him the time of day, frequently refusing even to look at him. Their treatment of him elicited resentment and mockery, and he lashed out in the stanzas of his poems.

Edwin A. chose the "ottava rima" style of mock-epic poem to structure his one-hundred-page titular poem, *A Walk Through Vicksburgh*. In the poem, he calls women "toads," "idiots," "creatures," "simpletons," "pig-faced" and "empty heads." He uses sarcasm abundantly, describing women as "modest beauties," "angels," "Southern belles" and, most frequently, "ladies."

The women seemed to be reliably repulsed by him—they refused to acknowledge his presence, or worse, acted rudely, gave him nasty looks and laughed at him behind his back. (In his words, they "deal behind you in a rude horse laugh"). And of course, they committed a worse crime: they chose other men over him. Frequently, Edwin A. derided the "seducers, duelists, and gamblers—brand the offals of the earth—the LIVING DAMN'D" whom Vicksburg women seemed to prefer over him. "The modest handsome gentleman gives place unto the bold, who 'smile to betray,'" he wrote.

Eating at a plantation home, Edwin A. observed that Vicksburg women acted like "abbesses" who "know, and feel, their station." While at the dinner table, a group of four ladies would not even acknowledge him, even though he "tried repeatedly to catch their eyes."

When he visited the Presbyterian church in Vicksburg, he was treated similarly. When he sat down at a pew, a woman "strained" to keep her eyes from him and pulled her dress away from him as if he were "infected."[44]

"For a young lady to notice you as if you were a human being is vastly ungenteel," he wrote.

When meeting women in the street, Edwin A. noted that they frequently reacted by "placing a parasol before their faces" and turning away. "The

Fashion plates showing women's fashion in 1846. *Metropolitan Museum of Art.*

ridiculous maneuver is insulting," he wrote. "A man doubtless is a very vulgar animal to a lady (I mean when he is not in the ballroom)." He compared women, sarcastically, to "houries," the maidens with beautiful eyes who, according to Islamic tradition, await faithful men in paradise.

Edwin A. did a lot of observing on the street, and it's another target for his repeated ridicule. The streets of Vicksburg in 1843–44 were apt to get so muddy, Edwin A. wrote, that losing a shoe was a distinct possibility on any given day. This is despite the fact that the city spent a large portion of its time and money on maintaining the streets; in the minutes of a January 1843 city council meeting, many of the items the city addressed involved fixing streets.[45]

Edwin A. complained that when riding in the country, the young women "gabber without even a decent recognition"—in other words, they completely ignored him. "What a difference in places north where I have been, the farmer's daughter would so pester you with their attention, that the roughest of us would blush considerable," he wrote. Another theme in Edwin A.'s poem: everything is better "down east."

The ratio of men to women in Vicksburg did not help Edwin A.'s chances. The Warren County census from 1840 shows that for every white woman in Vicksburg aged fifteen to thirty, there were 1.71 similarly aged white men. The numerical imbalance meant that Edwin A. was far from the only young man with no prospect of finding a female partner.[46]

Edwin A. was what we might call today an "involuntarily celibate," or a member of the "incel" community. In 2021, researchers at the International Center for the Study of Violent Extremism published the largest-ever study on the incel phenomenon. "Incels see themselves as involuntarily celibate because they feel undesirable and excluded from engagement in romantic or sexual liaisons," the study reads. "The incel community operates almost completely online and provides an outlet for members to express anger, frustration and blame toward women and society at large for feeling that they fail to include them in the prospect of sexual contact and partnership."

The description fits Edwin A. fairly well. He was depressed, lonely and desirous of female companionship—but he held out little hope that he would find that companionship. He blamed society—Vicksburg and the people in it. A modern incel would vent on an online forum; Edwin A. vented in his poem. A modern incel would hide his identity with an anonymous username; Edwin A. hid his identity by refusing to give his last name (and by, perhaps, using a pseudonym).

THE KISSER

At the same time that women slighted and insulted him, Edwin A. worshiped women—at least, an ideal of women—and frequently expressed his desire for companionship, both romantic and sexual. "I do love them, body, heart and soul," he wrote in one stanza.[47]

In his absence, Edwin A. apparently romanticized the women "down east." Their "sunny smiles" and "heavenly" conversation made "the cup of ecstasy run o'er." But "thou art many miles from those transcendent ones, I half adore." Edwin A.'s ideal woman was modest, compassionate, emotional, obedient and had "cheeks that oft do blush."[48]

Though Edwin A. expressed the desire for companionship in the idealistic sense, his stanzas are also frequently laden with sexual frustration. He reminisced about the time, years before, when he kissed a woman. The woman could be Ellen, to whom he dedicates a separate poem:

> *When in yonder bow'r I met thee*
> *Light hearted, cheeks all ruddiness;*
> *Thought you, I could e'er forget thee,*
> *Or that stolen rapturous kiss?*

Edwin A. expressed a persistent desire to kiss women—an act that he says is taboo in the South (men's mouths are always covered in tobacco juice, he explains). He evaluates women's mouths as being kissable or not. He remembered a woman in New Jersey from the past who had "the prettiest mouth imaginable, though her lips were chapped by the cold." The woman "sighed for a kiss," but Edwin A. didn't divulge whether he actually kissed her.[49]

Though he seldom had anything nice to say about the women he observed in Vicksburg, it does seem that he was smitten with a "sweet nymph," another anonymous poet in the city. He thought her poems were original and "exceeding[ly] beautiful," full of "pow'r, beauty, genius, brilliancy and fire" and "melancholy sweetness." And he imagined kissing her, though not on the lips: "For, dear madam, I would kiss your big toe, before the lips of beauties here below."[50]

An Irishwoman in town, a Catholic "beauty, shining like a star," caught the author's eye. He wrote that he'd like to pray to her, though "she would protest, 'tis likely, against me, or go perhaps, into a nunnery."[51]

VIEW OF VICKSBURG, MISSISSIPPI.

Depiction of antebellum Vicksburg, from *Ballou's Pictorial* (1855). *Library of Congress.*

Edwin A. was so moved by the sight of a young woman's cleavage that he wrote an entire poem called "To a Young Woman, Who Wore Her Dress Extremely Low on the Breast and Shoulders." In the poem, Edwin A. described, perhaps sarcastically, the sight of the woman's breasts: "Moulded with perfect grace / nature's purest clay / Expos'd to view! So white, so fair, what lily can with it compare?" Though he ended the poem with an admonition ("'tis shame to bare a part / provoking thoughts unclean"), it's clear the sight of her cleavage made a deep impression on him.[52]

"How thought of love the youthful bosom warms!" he wrote in another stanza. "To hold heav'ns masterpiece within our arms!"[53]

Edwin A. imagined spending nights with a woman in "Christian Intercourse":

> *Oh, might I nestle in some quiet place, where this fond fluttering heart would be at rest.... Then the twilight hours would not all run to waste— but in sweet converse be entirely blest: the bliss, that Christian intercourse bestows! The love, that on her sainted features glows!*[54]

Though Edwin A. was frequently ignored by Vicksburg women, when one did show interest in him, his confidence faltered. When one buxom widow "gazes" at him, he shrinks: "for fear of failure, I shall not advance."

WHAT ARE VICKSBURG WOMEN LIKE, ACCORDING TO EDWIN A.?

Overall, Edwin A. judged Vicksburg women to be "inferior in form—in soul—in majesty—in grace," despite the reputation Southern women had for being "an angel race." Vicksburg women lacked moral conviction and piety, according to him. They should have been protesting Vicksburg's culture of dueling, gambling and slavery. Instead, they spent their time pursuing "the amusements and recreations of polite society," leaving each a "tame and simple creature" in a state of perpetual lust and indolence. Each had a bad temper, and none could compose poetry (save for the nymph), socialize properly (have high-minded conversation) or bestow (on Edwin A.) affection. Vicksburg women gave their attention to the sons of enslavers, for whom the author had immense resentment. "And yet many here will jump at a man, however immoral, if he has the negroes," he wrote.[55]

Edwin A. seemed irritated by the contradictory behavior of Vicksburg women. They sometimes affected extreme modesty, covering their faces with parasols or refusing to acknowledge the presence of a male dinner guest. At other times they behaved ostentatiously. The author wrote that "some love to show themselves, as at a fair," and ride through Vicksburg alone, driving a horse at top speed, hair blowing in the wind. The clouds of dust such a woman raised functioned to draw even more attention to her. Male onlookers gaped at these women—before being consumed by the dust clouds.

Most Vicksburg women were "good for nothing," in Edwin A.'s estimation, while a few were "very good." The good-for-nothings were the women who "ogle, giggle, wriggle, and all that," repeated "stale, sniveling balderdash" and pat phrases, and who, of course, slighted Edwin A. The very good women numbered vastly fewer and could converse, rather than simply chat.

Though Edwin A. came off as judgmental and resentful toward many citizens of Vicksburg, he did display a strong sense of right and wrong when it came to the treatment of enslaved people and of the practice of slavery in general. He considered slavery an abominable, corrupting institution that rotted Southern society from within.

He was appalled by the violence that was casually carried out against the enslaved population of Vicksburg and its surroundings. While staying with a family in Louisiana, he observed a tall young woman cover her face in modesty while serving coffee and cornbread—and later beat an enslaved girl with a wooden plank until she "squalled considerable."

"Slavery annihilates the gentleness and tenderness connatural to the female heart," he wrote. "I have seen many striking proofs."

Edwin A. commented on "amalgamation"—sex between white men and Black women. He wrote that it is a common occurrence, with white men (or in his words, "the mass of men, from ev'ry clime and nation") taking a "when in Rome" approach to the practice of sex with enslaved women. "It must be laughable to Southern ladies, to read the frequent denunciations of this thing in their papers, while there are so many pledges squalling around them," he wrote. "And when they know that a good-looking yellow girl rarely, or never, escapes pollution—even if married. It is next to impossible for single men to be chaste here, such is the climate. Many buy good-looking girls for their pleasure."

George "Yankee" Hill. *Library of Congress.*

Vicksburg women liked to socialize and frequently attend public events. Edwin A. noted that Vicksburg women enjoyed ten-pin bowling, "while their shrill voices through the alley rings." They liked to travel to Brandon, "famous for her many sins," and to Mississippi Springs, a resort in Hinds County that could accommodate hundreds of visitors and whose water was claimed to cure virtually all diseases.[56] They delighted in attending barbecues. Afterward, they relished in the "bran dance." C.W. Webber, writing in 1858, described the dance this way: "[It was] a grand dance upon the rolled earth, sprinkled with bran beneath the arbors—and in which everybody, high or low, participated with a reckless abandon of jollity."[57]

Women loved going to the theater, where they were appraised and complimented by "fops." They wore fancy dresses and silk scarves and showed off gold Lepine pocket watches and diamond rings.

Southron's Hall on Washington Street was a popular venue for all sorts of social events. Southron's hosted cotillion parties, concerts of pianists, brass bands and singers, dances and even an exhibition of Queen Victoria's portrait.

The high rate of theater attendance irked Edwin A., who found it "remarkable" that so many Southern women attended theaters and balls compared to women in New England. He wrote about attending a Bible

Society meeting in Vicksburg. He was confused that there were fewer than a dozen attendees. After leaving, he understood—he passed by Southron's Hall, where the comedian Yankee Hill was performing. The venue was packed.

Edwin A. held the Methodists in low regard and considered Catholics superstitious. He viewed Methodists as sinners who hunted, fished, drank, chased runaways, went out for elaborate meals on the Sabbath and gathered en masse at noisy camp meetings. "Some get converted regularly every season, but the strong desire to shoot a runaway, see a horse-race, go to a ball, or 'feed the tiger' soon plunges them into the slough of rascality," he wrote.

Vicksburg's Embrace

Shortly before publishing his book, Edwin A. left Vicksburg on a riverboat and said farewell to the land of "gelid heart and pallid faces."

"I'd rather blow up here, with none to pity, than die a natural death, in Vicksburgh city," he wrote as the paddlewheel of his riverboat churned.

In the north, he looked forward to finding "those that do love me constant, true, and kind."

Edwin A. did not find much love in Vicksburg. But when he passed the packed Southron's Hall on the night of the Bible Society meeting, he may have felt a particularly painful sting, for Vicksburg had turned out in droves to see George Handel "Yankee" Hill, a Boston-born comedian whose whole schtick was acting the part of the "typical Yankee."

Yankee Hill's character was, as one scholar put it, "simple in the sense that he's unaffected." But behind his simple façade was a keen awareness—a cleverness that helped him turn situations to his favor. Others looked down on him, but he always came out on top. He was a plain man from "down east" whose outward appearance belied an inner intelligence. The premise must have seemed familiar to Edwin A. But for this Yankee, the people of Vicksburg had showed up in droves.

They seemed to be saying to Edwin A. that night, "We will not only shower a poor Yankee with attention; we will shower him with money. Make no mistake, Edwin—it's not me, it's you."

4

THE SIEGE OF VICKSBURG

General John Bowen Meets a Soldier's Death

Men don't want to starve, and don't intend to, but they call upon you for justice, if the commissary department can give it; if it can't, you must adopt some means to relieve us very soon. If you can't feed us, then you had better surrender us, horrible as the idea is, than suffer this noble army to disgrace themselves by desertion. I tell you plainly, men are not going to lie here and perish, [even] if they do love their country terribly. You had better heed a warning voice, though it is only the voice of a private soldier.
—Anonymous letter to Vicksburg Commander General John Pemberton, June 28, 1863[58]

JULY 2, 1863

General John Pemberton queried his four division commanders: Can the Vicksburg garrison hold on or make an escape, or is surrender advisable? All four concurred: get the best terms possible.

Pemberton agreed and chose General John Bowen to approach Grant under the white flag to ask for terms. A Pennsylvanian charged with defending Confederate Vicksburg, Pemberton gambled that Grant would have a strong incentive to complete the surrender by July 4. To sweeten his request, Pemberton sent Bowen, who had known and befriended Grant when the two lived in the same St. Louis neighborhood.

Nevertheless, Bowen's task would be both onerous and impractical. He hoped to surrender the Confederate army with honors and with all the soldiers paroled. Ulysses S. Grant only accepted one kind of surrender: unconditional. Pemberton was sending Bowen on a fool's errand if he expected clemency.

Still, he hoped Bowen could accomplish the unlikely, as he had done so many times the previous two years.

General Bowen arose that morning determined to perform the odious but necessary task of proposing surrender to his old friend. Bowen had been captured before, released and then seriously wounded at Shiloh, only to recover and save the Confederate army at the Second Battle of Corinth. Promoted and sent south to Grand Gulf, Bowen foresaw that Grant would cross the Mississippi River below Vicksburg at Grand Gulf. His pleas for reinforcements went unheeded. Still, he managed to delay a much superior army while placing himself repeatedly in harm's way. And when Grant sacked Jackson and turned west toward Vicksburg, it was Bowen who likely would have defeated Grant at Champion's Hill had any other division supported him. And it was Bowen who covered Pemberton's retreat into Vicksburg, where he followed and manned the works that cost Grant so many thousands of troops.[59]

In short, General John Bowen was the exemplar of a soldier. He personified

General John C. Pemberton. *Library of Congress.*

what war was supposed to be: romance, courage and glory. His men adored him. His wife left her two children behind in St. Louis with her mother to travel with her husband on his campaigns. Even his wounds were a minor setback.

General Bowen was Mars incarnate.

Bowen approached his old neighbor at 10:00 a.m. on that humid morning. He knew his enemy's reputation. Having faced Grant in battle, he knew his adversary's abilities. He was about to meet face to face with the man who would earn the sobriquet the "Butcher."[60]

What Bowen couldn't know was that a far deadlier foe had already entered Vicksburg. A fifth column was making plans to destroy thousands of soldiers and Bowen himself.

Bowen presented Grant with the following message from Pemberton, prefaced with Pemberton's request that his army be immediately paroled upon surrender: "I make this proposition to save the further effusion of blood, which must otherwise be shed to a frightful extent."

In compliance with his reputation, Grant responded: "The useless profusion of blood you propose stopping by this course can be ended at any time you may choose, by an unconditional surrender of the city and garrison.…I do not favor the proposition of appointing commissioners to arrange terms of capitulation, because I have no terms other than those indicated above."[61]

Bowen then delivered his own verbal request. Would General Grant be willing to meet personally with General Pemberton later that afternoon between the lines?[62]

Grant consented, and Bowen, weary and racked with pain, returned to the Confederate lines.

Whereas most voting Vicksburg residents initially opposed secession on account of their city's location on the Mississippi River and its prosperous trading ties to the North, by late 1860, secession fever had swept the state. On January 9, 1861, Mississippi delegates voted 84–15 to form the independent State of Mississippi and, four weeks later, joined the Confederacy.

Now, war fever swept Vicksburg, as its white citizens eagerly looked forward to the struggle that would free them and protect their "property." Just as in the Mexican War one generation before, young and old white citizens flocked to their state's new flag—a magnolia tree on a white background with a smaller "bonnie blue" flag in the upper left, all surrounded by a red border.

Most were certain the war would be a quick one—and a glorious one. The city remembered the glories of the First Mississippi Rifles fifteen years before. They remembered the excitement of '46. They remembered the courage of Colonel Jeff Davis. They remembered Buena Vista and the honor heaped upon the returning heroes who had sent Santa Anna scurrying home.

They had forgotten the 347 soldiers who failed to return home. They overlooked the musket ball lodged in Davis's foot and the far more serious wounds their returned veterans still carried. The scars on those honored and feted soldiers lucky enough to return home had begun to fade. As so often happens, a difficult and sometimes traumatic time was looked back on fondly. In short, the horrors of the Mexican War were forgotten. Only the victories at Monterrey and Buena Vista were remembered by those who never had to endure the war's hardships, sickness and death.

The current war would be the next generation's turn to prove their mettle—1776, 1814, 1846, 1861.

Mark Twain claimed that Walter Scott was responsible for the Civil War.[63] Glorious war, with all its pomp and circumstance. Fields of glory. Knights in shining armor—or gray and butternut coats. And for the inevitable slain, a quick and painless death. Hundreds of thousands of Ivanhoes, Richard the Lionhearts and knights flocked to the standards of their confederated states, determined to win their share of the laurels of a quick and glorious war.

By 1863, especially for those in Vicksburg, the reality of war had not lived up to its romantic promises.

Two-thirds of all Civil War deaths were due to disease. Of those deadly diseases, diarrhea was the deadliest. The federal and Confederate armies combined for more than fifty thousand deaths on account of diarrhea.[64]

Unsanitary conditions and a poor diet both contributed to widespread diarrhea.

It is hard for a twenty-first-century American to comprehend the terror of a liquid discharge. Today, an oral rehydration tablet or a Gatorade often solves the problem. People simply don't die of diarrhea today. That was not the case 150 years ago, when a wet bowel movement might mean death. If a person were at home, clean water, good food and rest likely cured the condition. A soldier on campaign, especially on the march, however, did not have those luxuries.

Nor did those forced to endure a forty-six-day siege in Mississippi during the summer months.

The horrors of the Vicksburg siege have been well documented. Over 1,600 soldiers lost their lives. Another 6,000 were wounded, many permanently. The citizens suffered daily and nightly terrors as shells and bullets filled the air. Most relocated to caves for safety. Food grew scarce.

Just as debilitating as hunger was sickness. And perhaps the worst sickness was the chronic diarrhea that affected so many on both sides. It has been estimated that of the 2.5 million Union soldiers, nearly 2 million suffered

General Ulysses S. Grant in 1863. *Library of Congress.*

from diarrhea during the war.[65] With more poverty and fewer resources as the war progressed, it can be assumed that Confederate numbers were higher. One study of the Vicksburg Campaign claims 1 in 10 federal soldiers and 1 in 7 Confederates were hospitalized and declared unfit for duty due to diarrhea.[66] As one surgeon claimed, "No matter what else a patient had, he had diarrhea."[67]

The siege of Vicksburg increased the cases of diarrhea and intensified its effects. Both sides were generally aware of the causes of diarrhea and made what plans they could to limit its occurrences and severity. Union soldiers—and Confederate to a lesser extent—were given desiccated vegetables to supplement their diet of pork, beans, coffee and hardtack or cornbread. Green beans, turnips, carrots, beets and onions were smashed into a footlong rectangular brick, one inch thick, and delivered to the soldiers, who were advised to boil it into a soup. (While a balanced diet with plenty of vegetables is a good preventative to diarrhea, the boiling process boiled the needed nutrients out of the vegetables. And yet, soup was the only palatable medium for many of the soldiers. Most would agree with a sergeant of the Fifteenth Iowa who wrote, "I ate a lot of desiccated vegetables yesterday and they made me the sickest of my life. I shall never want any more such fodder.")[68]

At least the Iowan had access to vegetables. His compatriots in the North held Sanitation Commission fairs where citizens were encouraged to donate and send vegetables to the boys in blue. One campaign encouraged attendees: "Don't send your sweetheart a love letter. Send him an onion."[69] As Grant's soldiers were bogged down outside Vicksburg, a vegetable shortage threatened to derail his campaign. More and more soldiers were falling ill, and diarrhea was rampant. Relief came in the form of the ladies of the Western Sanitary Commission, who collected and shipped the much-needed vegetables to Grant's army. While the U.S. Navy attempted to pound Vicksburg into submission, the "potato fleet" helped keep the U.S. Army in the field.

No such relief came to Vicksburg once Grant invested the city on May 18, 1863.

As Grant's noose tightened, sanitation loosened. Throughout the war, maintaining a sanitary camp was of paramount importance—and difficult to enforce. As one army surgeon explained: "Men were in the habit of going out into the bushes, and not infrequently some 30 or 40 feet from some of their tents and relieving themselves; in fact, human excrement has been promiscuously deposited in every direction, until the atmosphere… is so heavily loaded with effluvia that [it] is sickening."[70] Naturally, tired, demoralized men living in trenches for weeks at a time felt even less incentive to obey orders regarding sanitation. Add to exhaustion, malnourishment, sleeplessness and irritability, and the results were predictable. Hospitals filled, and fluid-filled bowels emptied.

For many, the excretion proved deadly. The death of a prisoner at Cahaba Prison in Alabama is typical of the manner in which so many Civil War soldiers died. Not only was death by diarrhea embarrassing, but it was also slow and agonizing. Jesse Hawes of the Ninth Illinois recorded the death of one of his comrades and fellow prisoners.

> *A tall young boy* [from Illinois made regular trips to the latrine. Days later,] *his journeys were as frequent, but his steps were slower, his face more hollow, his eyes more dull. He growled at first, then complained in a hollow voice; the lines of pain and long-suffering deepened on his face; his steps grew slower, weaker, sometimes staggering; he neglected to fasten his clothing; faeces ran from the bowels as he slowly dragged himself to the "sink." A day later he sat all day resting his chest upon his knees, his head falling forward. The next day he lay upon his side on the ground; some one gave him all he had; some boughs of pine for a bed. He was too weak to go to the "sink" now. The drawn, haggard, suffering face showed less of the agony he manifested a few days before, and more of weakness, dullness. The eyes grew more sunken, the discharges from the bowels were only a little bloody mucus. He could answer questions if one asked him anything; he asked occasionally for a sip of water, never for food. He was getting more and more stupefied. During the day we placed over him whatever we could to render him as comfortable as possible. I went to him in the night as he was only a few feet away from us and found him dead.*[71]

General Grant and General Pemberton discuss the terms of Vicksburg's surrender (1894). *Library of Congress.*

Hawes survived Cahaba and ended up being part of a prisoner exchange in 1865, when he was paroled in Vicksburg.

For Vicksburg residents, the 1861 dream of a glorious and romantic war had devolved into a nightmare just two years later. Most wars do. Historian Alan Huffman offers a clever disputation regarding the romance of war.

> *Even today, nearly a century and a half later, when Civil War reenactors stage cinematic mock battles and encampments, diarrhea is not a prominent feature of the historical play. The reenactments lack the awful details of rotting horse carcasses, camps ringed by cesspools, fistfights, and other troubling facts of life for men who endured being crowded together in a succession of rank and hostile environments for months at a time. There are no piles of amputated arms and legs outside the faux surgeons' tents, no disturbing stains on the seats of the soldiers' pants, no reenactors salving saddle sores or high-stepping to the woods. Somewhere, out of sight, there is toilet paper.*[72]

Less than five hours after his desperate mission to Grant, General John Bowman returned, this time with Vicksburg's commander, General Pemberton. Grant and his party waited at the designated locale outside Vicksburg's defenses.

The two sides exchanged greetings.

And then awkward silence.

More silence ensued, as neither side wished to speak first and thus cast themselves in the role of a supplicant.

Finally, Pemberton spoke, saying he had arrived at Grant's request to discuss the fate of Vicksburg.

Grant had made no such request. Bowen requested the meeting, and Grant agreed, assuming Pemberton was prepared to surrender.

Both looked to Bowen, who acknowledged his role in arranging the meeting.

Pemberton asked if Grant's terms remained the same. Grant confirmed, whereupon Pemberton turned to leave before turning back to Grant and promising that many, many more federal soldiers would be buried before Grant took Vicksburg, as he inevitably would. Pemberton's rant became

The Vicksburg Canal, by Adalbert John Volck (1860s). *Metropolitan Museum of Art.*

more vitriolic, and Grant realized that the doomed Confederate would make good on his word and bring down countless bluecoats with him.

Grant suggested that he and his counterpart step away from the others and discuss the situation in the shade of a neighboring oak tree.

Shortly after, the meeting adjourned, and Pemberton and Bowen returned to Vicksburg with a promise from Grant that the Confederates would receive his counteroffer by 10:00 p.m.

At the appointed hour, "Unconditional Surrender" Grant submitted his offer: Vicksburg's garrison would surrender the town in the morning, and all soldiers would be immediately paroled.

Pemberton accepted the offer.

Grant's genius, Pemberton's gamble and Bowen's foresight had all paid off. Those still living would continue to do so—all but a handful.

General Bowen recognized the symptoms. A pain in his stomach. Weakness. Brownish water in the latrine. His staff, too, recognized the dreaded sickness. Bowen's wife, who was staying eighteen miles away in Edwards, was summoned. So was his priest. It was hoped that with prayer, luck and medical attention, the general might be saved. His entourage decided to move him east to Raymond for treatment.

On July 12, after suffering for more than a week with diarrhea, Bowen; his priest, Father John Bannon; and wife, Mary, boarded an ambulance and headed east. Eight miles from Raymond, it became clear that General Bowen was dying. The ambulance stopped at the nearest house in a last desperate attempt to revive the general. The home's overseer suggested traveling to another house just two miles farther, where Bowen would be more comfortable. The party acquiesced. They moved to a house down the road. That night, Father Bannon wrote in his journal: "July 12, Gen. Bowen was too sick to move any further."[73] The Catholic priest, who had given last rites and buried so many over the previous two years, sensed the inevitable. His prognostication of doom was fulfilled by morning. General John Bowen was dead.

The man who had defied the odds at Shiloh, Corinth and Vicksburg, who had maintained his health until the last week of the siege of Vicksburg, was buried in an impromptu coffin without even the screws to secure the top. With his wife, priest and a few onlookers present, he was buried in the garden of the house in which he died.[74]

General John Bowman was one of the 620,000 lives claimed by the Civil War and one of the 57,000 to die in the arms of the Valkyrie, wet feces leaking down her gown.

5

THE *SULTANA*

America's Deadliest Boat

Ann Annis was jolted awake by the loud rattling of iron. Her husband looked out their private stateroom aboard the *Sultana* and saw a cloud of steam rapidly approaching. He slammed the door shut and tried to leave by another. It was jammed. Thinking quickly, he placed a life preserver over himself and his wife, grabbed his seven-year-old daughter, Isabella, still in her pink nightgown her mother had bought her, and darted toward the ship's stern, where he tied one end of a rope to the ship's bridge and tossed the other into the Mississippi River. Instructing Ann to follow and Isabella to jump on his back, Harvey began to lower himself into the frigid Mississippi River. Ann followed, determined to keep her family together, but just then, a man on the deck above leaped off, knocking Ann onto the hold of the ship. Terrified of losing her husband and child, Ann rose and leaped into the Mississippi River.[75]

Ann knew the pain of losing a husband. She had already lost two. And she knew the panic of being lost at sea. She had been before.

Ann Vessey married Captain James Laird at the end of 1840. Six months later, on her first sea voyage with her captain-husband, Ann was stranded at sea when Laird's ship sank off the coast of England. Laird and most of the passengers drowned, but fortunately for Ann and a handful of survivors, the

Union veteran U.D. Wood, a native of Wisconsin, photographed in the 1890s. *Library of Congress.*

wreck occurred near a small island, to which they floated and swam. After being marooned for three days, Ann and what was left of her companions were rescued by a passing ship.

Undaunted by marriage to a seaman, Ann quickly married a second captain in 1842. Three children and seven years later, he, too, was lost at sea. Perhaps hoping to escape life in England, with its concomitant reminders of the sea, Ann, her parents and her three children set sail for America. Upon arrival, they immediately made their way to Wisconsin, where, within a year, Ann was once again married.

The next decade was presumably a time of contentment for Ann Annis, the wife of Harvey Annis. The couple would raise four more children—in addition to the three Ann had brought into the marriage—and Ann, as events would later demonstrate, seemed to be quite devoted to her third husband.

But in 1861, a thousand miles away in Charleston, South Carolina, shots were fired into the same Atlantic Ocean that claimed her first two husbands, and Ann's life would be permanently altered. It seemed as if her fate was irrevocably bound to the water.

Harvey Annis enlisted in the Union army. By 1864, he had risen to the rank of second lieutenant and was placed with the Fifty-First U.S. Colored Infantry. The regiment was sent to help defend the newly captured Vicksburg. There, Harvey Annis fell seriously ill with an enlarged spleen and the ever-dangerous diarrhea.

Word reached Ann, who understood the seriousness of the diagnosis. She left her eldest daughter in charge of her still-homebound children and departed for Vicksburg with her youngest, seven-year-old, Isabella, or Belle.

Ann took personal charge of her husband and soon nursed him back to health. In February 1865, Harvey resigned his commission and immediately began making plans to take Ann and Belle back to Oshkosh to reunite with the rest of their family. He booked passage aboard a comfortable 370-passenger steamboat, the *Sultana*. To ensure his family's comfort, the second lieutenant rented a private stateroom on the *Sultana*.[76]

The Boarding

Harvey and Ann were eager to return to their family in Wisconsin. Harvey booked passage on the steamboat *Sultana* and, as an officer, was given a private stateroom. Harvey, Ann and Belle would travel comfortably to Cairo, Illinois, and then take a train the last leg of the way.

Unknown to the Annises, one of the *Sultana*'s four high-pressure boilers had sprung a small but dangerous leak about seventy-five miles south of Vicksburg. The ship was forced to dock at Natchez for repairs and then again at Vicksburg. The stop at Vicksburg proved necessary (to again repair the boiler) but also potentially lucrative, for thousands of recently paroled Union prisoners awaited passage back home. This promised to be quite a boon for steamship owners, as the federal government was paying a stipend of five dollars for each Union soldier and ten dollars for each officer transported home.

Captain Cass Mason, who, with five partners, had just bought the two-year-old *Sultana* for $80,000, saw a way to make his boat pay for itself early: he would make his usual run to New Orleans and, on the way back, load his boat with former prisoners. Of course, other steamboat captains had similar ideas. The parleying for the available human cargo contracts would likely prove intense.[77]

The boiler leak threatened to ruin Mason's plans.

As soon as the *Sultana* docked in Vicksburg on April 23, Captain Mason ordered repairmen to get to work. The leak was covered by a two-foot-by-one-foot sheet of metal that was a quarter of an inch thick. Major repairs would be put off until they arrived in St. Louis and the majority of their parolees disembarked. The plan might work, as long as the superheated water did not explode through the quarter-inch sheet of metal and the boat did not careen and open air pockets that could cause an explosion of boiling water and steam.[78]

The repair to the boiler was made, and the *Sultana* entered negotiations for quite a profitable passenger list.

The *Sultana* was licensed to carry 376 passengers. When it docked in Vicksburg, it already had about half that number. Mason could legally take on about another 200 parolees. But other boats had recently departed the prison camp at Vicksburg with overloaded boats. Mason wanted in on the action.

Technically, Assistant Adjutant General Frederick Speed was in charge of distributing the prisoners to the eager steamboat captains. (Most of the

The overloaded *Sultana*, photographed in Helena, Arkansas, the day before it sank. *Library of Congress.*

prisoners had been recently released from Confederate prison camps, most notably, the notorious Andersonville. Needless to say, they were eager to return home as soon as possible.) But Mason preferred to deal with Colonel Reuben Hatch, the chief quartermaster. It was a wise decision if money was Mason's motivation.

Hatch was a thrice disgraced officer who had been court-martialed for several instances of embezzlement. Just two months before, he was declared "totally unfit" to serve as quartermaster. However, Hatch's brother was a close friend of President Lincoln, who personally interceded to see the charges against Hatch were dropped and that he was sent to Vicksburg. Upon arrival, Hatch immediately resumed his scheming. He cut a deal with Mason to fill up the *Sultana* with parolees on the ship's return trip from New Orleans.

When the *Sultana* docked on April 23, Mason visited Hatch and was told there would be a bureaucratic delay. Incensed, Mason went to Steed's office and demanded his human cargo. Speed acquiesced and agreed to send all remaining parolees to the *Sultana*.

Meanwhile, two more steamboats headed north arrived and docked next to the *Sultana*. Yet Steed was determined to keep his word. Mason had agreed to accept a bulk rate of three dollars per head in exchange for the contract.[79] (Where the remaining two dollars per head ended up is unknown.)

The prisoners boarded a train at the sight of their exchange near Vicksburg and, an hour later, arrived at the docks. The first batch was sent aboard the *Sultana*. And the next batch. And the next. And so on. A second train arrived while the two other steamships waited alongside the *Sultana*. But these parolees, too, were sent to the *Sultana*. All of them. When a third train arrived with paroled soldiers, even Captain Mason became concerned. He told Steed he could take aboard no more. Steed ignored his plea. The loading continued. Another detachment of soldiers came aboard. And then another. Mason stood on the gangway and claimed he would take no more. He was ignored as still more soldiers boarded. Finally, the last of the parolees crowded onto the *Sultana*. All 2,400.

Surprised—and likely disappointed in missing the handling fees— one of the two steamboats docked next to the *Sultana* sailed away with seventeen passengers.[80]

The *Sultana*'s 2,600 passengers and crew soon followed.

The excited and eager Annises boarded the *Sultana* on April 24, thoughts of children and siblings no doubt at the front of their minds. They watched as equally excited passengers boarded, most also on their way home after a long absence. And then more boarded. And more. And still more. A concerned Harvey pointed out the sagging deck to an officer, who promptly assured him the ship was not overloaded. Later, Ann testified, "Great fear was felt by everybody on account of the large number of passengers and the boat being top heavy. The clerk or mate pointed out to my husband and myself the sagging down of the hurricane deck in spite of extra stanchions which were put in a great many places. The boat was very much crowded, but the men behaved very well indeed."[81]

The journey, though crowded, proceeded peacefully and uneventfully. (One of the few inconveniences being the difficulty of accessing the toilets—a particular problem to the many soldiers still suffering from chronic diarrhea.)[82] After a full night on the river, nerves due to the overcrowding would have waned. Besides, the crowds would have been little concern to Ann, for she had her own stateroom and would only occasionally have ventured forth, if at all. If she did, she might have seen the alligator the crew kept as a pet and who entertained the fascinated crowd, many of whom had never seen an alligator. She might also have seen a show put on by the Chicago Opera Troupe, who rode the *Sultana* on their way to Memphis.[83] Mostly, she would have looked forward to reuniting with her family.

The *Sultana* arrived at Helena, Arkansas, at 7:00 a.m. April 26. After a one-hour stop, the boat continued on to Memphis, reaching the port that evening. Some passengers—including the Chicago Opera Troupe— disembarked only to be replaced by others. At 10:30 a.m., the signal bell announced its impending departure. The *Sultana* picked up a load of coal across the river on the Arkansas side and at 1:00 a.m. on Thursday, April 27, the steamboat set out for Cairo, Illinois.

Forty-five minutes later, the *Sultana* entered a broad stretch of the Mississippi River, five frigid miles wide due to the recent flooding.[84]

⸎

The Explosion

The following morning, a local paper, the *Memphis Argus*, explained what happened next:

> *Having discharged the freight for this city, the Sultana proceeded on her way up the river, leaving our wharf at about 2 o'clock yesterday morning. When about seven miles above the city she exploded her boilers; the entire middle portion of the boat, including the texas and pilot house, was hurled high in the air and scattered over the water. Immediately after the explosion fire broke out; a vast volume of flame swept through the cabin from the front to the stern of the boat. Then ensured a scene which language cannot describe—the most terrible that can possibly be conceived.*
>
> *The explosion occurred in a wide portion of the river, there being no land for a mile on either side. Many were scalded to death immediately; those who were not injured were jumping overboard. The river for a mile around was full of floating people; the light of the burning boat shone over a scene such as has never before been witnessed; such as language cannot paint or imagination conceive. The screams of women, the groans of those who were wounded and thrown from the boat by the force of the explosion, the cries for help when there were none to assist—all contributed to create a scene over which we are compelled to shudder with horror.*

Ann and her family were not the only ones fighting to survive. Everyone was.[85] Any near-death scenario is likely to cause widespread panic, but death by drowning more so. Instincts kick in. Even the best of persons involuntarily panic and become unwilling weapons of death.

Drowning people will attempt to hold their breath when in water while they flail and fight to raise their head above water for oxygen. As they struggle,

Depiction of the *Sultana* burning, published in *Harper's Weekly* (1865). *University of Michigan Library.*

terror sets in, and the flailing uses up valuable oxygen in the bloodstream. Eventually, the biological reflex to exhale carbon dioxide and breathe air takes over, even when underwater. As water fills the airways, laryngospasm, a reflexive closing of the vocal cords, occurs to keep fluid out of the lungs. Still, oxygen is unable to go to the brain and either a loss of consciousness or cardiac arrest ensues.

For those aboard the *Sultana*, the frigid waters of the Mississippi River decreased their chance for survival. Many, immediately shocked by the coldness of the water, hyperventilated and took in too much water. Others tried treading water, floating or holding on to debris but quickly expired as their bodies began to reflexively shuttle blood from their extremities to their cores in a desperate attempt to save vital organs. With the major organs preserved, the arms and hands lost their ability to swim or grip impromptu life-preservers.

As the body temperature of those who survived the explosion dropped, their heart rates and blood pressure rose. Those who did not go into cardiac arrest then saw their blood pressures quickly drop—too quickly. Literally every minute, more and more survivors slipped into unconsciousness and a watery grave. The quickly dwindling number of survivors were in a race against time—a race most were losing.[86]

And then there was the battle against the Mississippi River itself. The Father of Waters is a generous, life-giving river that nourishes a continent. But it is also a dangerous and unpredictable river, and those dangers multiply during highwater. The Mississippi River, in April 1865, was not only in highwater, it was flooding. The already strong currents were moving faster—fast enough to push a person one hundred yards in just a minute. The floods had downed innumerable trees, creating eddies and whirlpools that would drown even the most experienced swimmer. Crosscurrents and whirlpools routinely sucked down massive floating trees and vomited them up again miles downstream. Few swimmers, even under ideal conditions, are able to last long in the Great River's powerful currents.[87]

Three survivors lived and told their harrowing tales of struggle and survival. Their stories exemplify the ordeals of the other passengers, some of whom survived. Most did not.

Union soldier W.A. Fast awoke when the boilers exploded. Thinking quickly, he pulled a door off its hinges and prepared to leap into the Mississippi. Just before doing so, he noticed "hundreds of people grasping for anything afloat, drowning each other en masse, after which there would be a brief intermission before the next group dove in." He quickly decided to wait for the latest batch to drown. But then more jumped in as the *Sultana*'s fires spread and the ship sank lower and lower. Still, Fast waited to make his irrevocable jump, as beneath him, people were "struggling, swimming, sinking. My plan was to stick to the boat as long as I could and until the swimmers were well out of my way."[88]

Finally, Fast leaped into the Mississippi with his door-raft. Enough passengers had drowned by then to increase his odds of survival.

Private Commodore Smith walked the deck in a state of anguish.[89] So many of the men were burning to death aboard, but they were too weak to throw themselves overboard. Either their recent imprisonment or injuries from the explosion had incapacitated them. Smith heard their pleas, their gut-wrenching prayers to be tossed overboard. Anything was better than being burned alive, even death by drowning.

Smith knew the water would be certain and near-immediate death for these pitiable men. He knew he would be committing assisted murder. But he knew that by doing nothing, he was condemning them to a worse fate.

Working with two other soldiers who later claimed they threw fifty wounded men overboard, Smith began tossing his comrades to their doom. Some men were scalded so badly that their skin peeled off as Smith lifted them. Still, he pushed them into the river that quickly became their grave. Later, he wrote that easing these men's passage was "the hardest task of my life…the most heartrending task human beings could be called upon to perform."[90]

Ohio Private William Lugenbeal decided to live no matter the cost. Nearly all the other passengers had made the same decision. But Lugenbeal had an advantage: he was thinking clearly.

The Ohioan swiftly made his way toward the alligator and stabbed the encaged animal three times with his bayonet before dragging the corpse out of its box. He then tossed the wooden box overboard, as far away from people as he could, and jumped in after it. He defended his box as if his life depended on it, for it did. "When a man would get close enough I would kick him off, then turn quick as I could and kick someone else to keep them from getting hold of me."[91] When he neared a drowning man, he passed on by, refusing to help anyone, knowing that by doing so, they both would likely die. When later asked about his heartless, callous actions that led to the deaths of so many, Lugenbeal replied, "What do you think you would do?"[92]

What do you think *you* would do?

<hr/>

Death and Survival

Ann hit the frigid water of the Mississippi and gasped. She struggled to stay afloat because her life-preserver was not attached properly. She grabbed the rudder, but the fire on the boat eventually burned the backs of her hands up to her shoulders and forced her to let go. She drifted off into the dark, cold Mississippi River.

Having lost sight of her husband and daughter, and with her life preserver useless, Ann struggled to remain afloat. She was quickly growing exhausted. At last, she grabbed at a piece of driftwood that was floating by, but a man was already clinging to it and pushed her off. The man, Corporal Albert King, drifted away, but he must have had a pained conscience—or else he figured a woman wasn't much of a threat and his driftwood could sustain the added weight—for he kicked his way back to Ann and allowed her to share his debris-raft.

The two drifted for hours. Ann was in hysterics over her separated husband and daughter. She continuously cried out for help. No help came, and the pair continued to drift down the dark, cold Mississippi River. Sheer

The Vicksburg courtroom where Frederick Speed was convicted but later pardoned for overloading the *Sultana*. *Joseph Starrett*.

exhaustion finally calmed Ann down. She had expended too much energy trying to stay afloat and shouting. The cold water caused her blood pressure to drop dangerously low. She was doomed to die like most of the other passengers. It was only a matter of time.

And then King's foot hit a submerged tree. Both he and Ann were able to stand on the tree, with only their heads above water. And then they waited. And waited.

At last, an Arkansas farmer, John Fogelman, rallied some neighbors, built a log raft, and set out at 8:00 a.m. to rescue what survivors they could. The prudent farmer was cautious to avoid large groups—not too many were left—and ferried fortunate passengers back to his house for warmth and what treatment he could offer. Back and forth, back and forth the rescue raft went until, at last, Fogelman came across a still-living Ann Annis and Albert King. Too cold to express much gratitude, the two were brought aboard the raft and taken to Fogelman's cabin, where they were given blankets and placed by a large bonfire.[93]

Freezing, traumatized and in a state of shock, Ann Annis had survived the greatest maritime disaster in United States history. Over 1,700 passengers never reached land again.[94]

The Aftermath

Ann Annis was taken to a military hospital in Memphis, where she was treated for shock and burns. Now warm and likely to survive, Ann begged anyone near for news of her husband and daughter. So great was her anxiety and trauma that she had to be heavily sedated. She drifted into unconsciousness with Harvey's and Belle's names on her lips.[95]

Ann remained at the hospital for more than a month as she recovered. While there, she learned that a soldier had seen a girl on a glass door or window drifting down the river. A man was clinging to the wood next to her. Another soldier claimed a girl atop a door with a man holding on passed between him and an eddy. The door drifted toward the eddy and began to spin. The girl fell off, and the man dove in after her. Neither rose again.

The girl had been wearing a pink dress.[96]

When Ann was able to move about again, she searched the city's morgues for the bodies of her husband and daughter, viewing hundreds of bodies killed by either steam or water. Finally, having lost all hope of returning their bodies to the family plot in Wisconsin, Ann made the long, lonely trek home.[97]

For the next thirty-five years, Ann wore long sleeves, even in summer, to cover the scars of her burns. She wore her scarred heart on those same sleeves, mourning the traumatic deaths of Harvey and Belle until the day she died.[98]

6

A WIFE, A WAR; ANOTHER WIFE, ANOTHER WAR

Jefferson Davis and Brierfield Plantation

LEXINGTON, KENTUCKY

June 17, 1835

Sarah Knox Taylor stood next to her fiancé in her aunt's house in Lexington, Kentucky. She was a long way from her father's fort in Wisconsin. It was in the untamed Northwest Territory[99] that she met Lieutenant Jefferson Davis, the man she would fall helplessly in love with, even to the point of defying her father and threatening to elope. Her beau reciprocated what was seen to be reckless love. Sarah and Jefferson believed her father and his commander, Colonel Zachary Taylor's, vehement objection to their union emanated from her father's wish that his daughter not be subjected to a soldier's life. After all, the crusty colonel had lost two daughters and nearly his wife to harsh conditions on the frontier. As an army wife, Sarah would spend years—and likely decades—on the move and constantly in danger. His daughter deserved better.[100]

In March 1835, Jefferson traveled to his brother Joseph's house on Davis Bend, where he told him of his desire to marry Sarah. Joseph suggested that he do just that. Leave the army, marry his ex-commander's daughter and come live with him on Davis Bend. The elder brother would set aside nine hundred acres adjoining his land, as well as money for sixteen enslaved people.[101] Jefferson would tame his own land, build his own house and spend his life alongside his esteemed brother.

Portrait of a younger Jefferson Davis, by William Washburn (1888). *Library of Congress.*

Jefferson did just as his brother advised. He returned to his post, resigned his commission and met Sarah at her aunt's house in Lexington, Kentucky, where the couple were married before her friends and family. Her disapproving father provided the newlyweds with a sizeable dowry.

Sarah and Jefferson immediately left for their honeymoon on a steamship headed toward their new home at Davis Bend.

Two weeks later, the couple arrived at Joseph's Hurricane Plantation, where they would stay until Jefferson could build his bride their own home.[102] Soon after arrival, Sarah accompanied her husband to see their new land. It was wild and untamed, covered in briars and brambles. But it was theirs. Their home. They accurately and affectionately named their estate Brierfield.[103]

Six weeks later, tragedy struck. Jefferson came down with malaria. The next day, Sarah developed chills and a fever. The newlyweds decided to leave the swampy lands around Hurricane and stay with Jefferson's sister near St. Francisville across the river until their fevers broke. Sarah continued to worsen, and one month later, she died in her husband's arms.

A distraught and widowed Jefferson Davis buried his young wife at his sister's home, and after a bout of depression in which he lost interest in his land, he finally returned, alone, to Hurricane.[104]

DAVIS BEND

1844–1845

Varina Howell was a fortunate woman. Her father was a good man who cherished his daughter. He was also close friends with Joseph Davis, who took William Howell under his wing and introduced the New Jersey transplant to Natchez society. Although Howell was never as successful as his good friend, the two developed a relationship that spanned both their lives.

Howell's connections enabled him to send Varina to a prestigious boarding school in Philadelphia. When she returned, Varina continued her education with Judge George Winchester of Natchez. She was the judge's only pupil and flourished under his tutelage, receiving an education available to few women.

In 1842, Joseph Davis invited the Howells to Hurricane Plantation for a visit. Varina, however, was so engrossed in her studies with Judge Winchester that she requested a rain check. It was granted, and she made her first trip to Hurricane to visit her "Uncle Joe" in December 1843.

It was a trip that altered her life in ways she could not imagine.

It was the first time she met Joseph's brother Jefferson Davis.

Varina's first impressions of Davis vacillated between timidity, respect and curiosity. She would write home to her mother that she was unable to determine Jefferson's age, as he seemed both youthful and aged at once. She found him "most agreeable [with] a peculiarly sweet voice and a winning manner of asserting himself." "He is the kind of person I should expect to rescue one from a mad dog at any risk, but to insist on a stoical indifference to the fright afterward." Though charmed, Varina also found fault with Davis, writing to her mother that he had "an uncertain temper, and…a way of taking for granted that everybody agrees with him when he expresses an opinion, which offends me."[105] Nevertheless, the first meeting between Varina and Jefferson sowed seeds that would bear unexpected fruit.

Jefferson asked his brother to arrange another meeting between him and Varina. Just as he had encouraged his brother with Sarah Taylor, so Joseph supported Jefferson now. He invited Varina to stay at Hurricane. She did so for two months, and for most of this time, Jefferson was also present.

The pair quickly escalated from curiosity to infatuation to passion. Varina now described Jefferson as "a very gay fellow…look[ing] about thirty; erect, well-proportioned, and active as a boy.…He rode with more grace than any man I have ever seen, and gave one the impression of being incapable either of being unseated or fatigued."[106] Jefferson was equally smitten. He soon proposed to the strong-willed eighteen-year-old. Varina reciprocated his love but wanted to talk with her parents first. Conscious of the age gap, Jefferson did not want to be perceived as pressuring the young would-be bride into a marriage and agreed to let her speak with her parents alone.

Varina did so and quickly overcame her mother's objections regarding her suitor's age and obvious affection for his first deceased wife, Sarah. Varina wrote to her now-fiancé and rejoicingly told him of her parents' approval.

Brierfield, the home of Jefferson Davis, on Davis Island, twenty miles downriver from Vicksburg. *Library of Congress.*

Until the day they were married, Jefferson bombarded his soon-to-be bride with letters of his love. Varina wrote back in equally ardent terms but asked her beloved to burn the letters. Jefferson replied, "If the house was on fire those letters with the flowers you have made sacred by wearing and the lock of your hair" would force him to dash back in at the risk of his life to retrieve them.[107] In a preview of events to come, Varina got her way. None of *her* love letters to Jefferson survive.

Still, Varina foresaw a potential source of conflict. She insisted on them having a place of their own, a place that would be Jefferson and Varina Davis's alone. In a letter, Jefferson reminded Varina that he was Joseph's brother. He would be her husband, but he was still—and would always be—Joseph's brother.

That dichotomy would threaten to destroy the relationship of Joseph, Jefferson and Varina.

Just as prescient as his fiancée, Jefferson wrote Varina the night before they exchanged vows, asking her to be patient with the situation in which she would soon find herself and promising to become the man she hoped to marry. He also asked her to sacrifice her own nature for the sake of a prosperous and happy marriage. "I wish you would put in that Lion pawing up the dirt, without which I fear you will find the picture incomplete."[108]

Little did Jefferson know, he was about to be standing between a lion and a lioness.

And he was about to learn just how uncomfortable that position could be. Jefferson and Varina were married on February 26, 1845.

MONTERREY, MEXICO

September 21, 1846

"Fire advancing!" Colonel Jefferson Davis was determined to take the Tannery, a fortified Mexican position that threatened to turn back the American attack. Davis's First Mississippians, along with their comrades from the First Tennessee, had advanced beyond the American lines. While Davis would have preferred an orderly, methodical advance that would have done justice to his West Point training, he was more determined to take the fortification, and he urged his men on from his horse: "Damn it, why don't the men get nearer the fort?" "Now is the time, Great God, if I had 30 men with knives I could take that fort!" His men, including his neighbors, the Vicksburg Volunteers, advanced in tens, eight, and fours, closer and closer; 110 yards away, 80, 30. Finally, at noon, the scattered regiments charged and took the Tannery. Private Joseph Davis Howell, a nephew of Jefferson Davis, claimed that "suddenly the order to charge was given by Col. Davis and away we went like so many devils hooting and yelling, with nothing but our naked rifles no bayonets even."[109]

Still, they advanced beyond the Tannery. Davis and sixty of his men waded beyond the waist-deep stream behind their initial objective, 150 yards into the city itself. They gathered behind a small hill and fence. The colonel from Vicksburg was prepared to take the next deadly Mexican position, the Ricon del Diablo. Perhaps ill-advisedly, perhaps fortunately, Davis and his men were ordered back. (Davis adhered to the former view in the immediate aftermath of the battle.)

After rallying separate Mississippi units, Colonel Davis next planned to capture the La Purisma Bridge. Again, he was ordered to stand down. Shortly after, all U.S. troops were ordered to withdraw from Monterrey. Davis reluctantly complied.

As the U.S. Army withdrew, some weary units lagged. Sensing blood, a unit of Mexican lancers rode out of Monterrey to add to the U.S. death count. Davis promptly marched his Mississippi troops back toward the city, where he scattered the lancers and saved the American stragglers.[110]

The Battle of Monterrey confirmed the United States as an international force. True, the United States had fought Great Britain to a standstill three decades before in the War of 1812 and had won numerous victories against a waning Spanish empire and Native tribes, but the Battle of Monterrey was fought against a waxing sovereign nation on their own territory, against troops who fought in the classic European style.

The battle also introduced Jefferson Davis, gentleman farmer, as a war hero. His nephew Joseph Howell wrote home to his father: "I verily believe that if he should tell his men to jump into a cannon's mouth they would think it alright & would all say Col. Jeff as they call him knows best so hurra [*sic*] boys lets [*sic*] go ahead."[111]

News reached Vicksburg of the battle. Joseph Davis eagerly read of the exploits of the First Mississippi and wrote his brother: "Yesterday we read accounts of the Battle of Monterey. You may easily imagine the feeling intense anxiety with which the news was read and listened to by all parties. I came to the list of killed and wounded, here my eyes failed me, my voice grew tremulous. But Heaven be praised you were not on the list."[112]

Not long after, Joseph would see his dear younger brother in person.

FURLOUGH

October 18–December 17, 1846

Jefferson and Varina stood among a crowd of people, saying their goodbyes. Each time Varina turned to go, Jeff ran back to her and kissed her lips. Over and over again.

At least that's how it happened in Varina's dream. "I actually waked with your kisses so warm upon my lips that I could not believe you were not in my arms. Dearest, best beloved, may God bring you these arms, and then at least for the time I clasp you I shall be happy."[113]

Things were not well on the home front. Davis thought he knew why.

A month after the Battle of Monterrey, Davis was granted a sixty-day furlough to visit his ailing wife. Two weeks later, he was home at Davis Bend after a three-month absence.

Varina had spent the previous three months living with Joseph Davis at Hurricane. The situation became untenable for the twenty-year-old wife and sixty-two-year-old brother-in-law. Joseph played the role of a paternalistic grandfather to the intelligent and independent woman. Varina already disapproved of the patronizing way she believed Joseph treated her husband. Varina frowned on any hint of dependency in her husband and herself.

Varina Davis, photographed during the Civil War. *Library of Congress.*

A lack of children after eighteen months of marriage no doubt added to Varina's frustration. Perhaps her husband's furlough from Mexico could rectify that emptiness.

Davis's brief return did provide one tangible boon for Varina. The recent newlyweds would be building their own house, near Joseph but far enough away to satisfy Varina. Once the house was built, she would finally be mistress of her own home.[114]

Davis's timely return to Vicksburg also magnified the heroic light in which he stood. Numerous Mississippians—Vicksburg citizens included—had performed well at Monterrey. But it was Jefferson Davis who now stood before his fellow citizens to tell them in person of the bravery of their fathers, sons, brothers and beaus. A verifiable war hero stood much to gain in any American state. In Mississippi, political success was a foregone conclusion.

Satisfied that the relationship had been patched up between his wife and brother, convinced that Varina was mollified by his brief return and promise to build her *her* own house and optimistic that his political star was waxing, Davis returned to his unit in Mexico after a month-long furlough in Vicksburg.

BUENA VISTA, MEXICO

February 22–February 23, 1847

Just two months after Davis rejoined his unit, his bravery was again on display. His former father-in-law and current commander, General Zachary Taylor, learned that Santa Anna was advancing on Taylor's new post, Saltillo, at the head of twenty thousand men. Outnumbered three to one and with only the First Mississippi having been in combat before, Taylor decided to stay and fight it out with the aggressive Mexican commander.

Taylor drew up his forces three miles south of Saltillo over a landscape littered with natural gullies, trenches and crevices. The scarred ground looked as if it had already been pounded into submission by centuries of repeated cannon blasts. Taylor would use the ground to his advantage, but his most important weapon that day ended up being Jefferson Davis and his First Mississippi Rifles.

At 8:00 a.m. on February 22, Santa Anna launched his assault. Within the hour, he had turned the American left flank and was threatening to overrun and route Taylor's entire force.

At that very moment, Davis arrived on the scene. Davis's men quickly filled their canteens at the nearby hacienda and then marched at the double quick, right at a full division of Mexican soldiers, Davis in front, atop his horse, shouting encouragement. Davis ordered his four hundred to charge Santa Anna's four thousand. When the First Mississippi got within musket shot range, Davis ordered his men to advance firing. They did, firing a total of twenty-one volleys into the tightly packed and stunned Mexicans. Santa Anna's regulars fled. The American route was forestalled.

The First Mississippi took up a defensive position. Only when they were finally reinforced by an Indiana regiment, did Davis look to his lower leg, which had been pierced by a musket ball. The ball had smashed his spur, sending metal and sock material into his leg, just above of his ankle. Despite the pain, Davis would not dismount. The battle was still in doubt.

A wounded Davis looked over the battlefield that still protected the American rear. Four hundred yards away and closing fast galloped two thousand Mexican lancers. Davis would later write that the "richly caparisoned lancers came forward rapidly and in beautiful order—the files and ranks so closed, as to look like a solid mass of men and horses."[115]

Davis's men had never been exposed to a cavalry charge. The normal, time-tested procedure would be to draw his men into a hollow square.

Davis hadn't the time. He aligned his men in a V, with the Indiana regiment and First Mississippi on either side, and he ordered his men to hold their fire until the cavalry was directly upon them. When the lancers trotted to within about fifty yards, they slowed to a walk, aligning themselves for a decisive charge that would scatter Davis's unit and turn the American flank. Suddenly a sprinkling of shots peppered the lancers. And then came a volley so devastating that the cavalry turned and fled en masse.

For the second time that day, Davis had saved the American flank. Still, the fight was not over, and Davis would be called on one last time to turn the tide of battle.

General Taylor, believing the Mexicans to be in retreat when Davis's V scattered the lancers, ordered an advance on Santa Anna's center. Santa Anna, still confident of victory, ordered an all-out assault on Taylor's center.

The result was predictable: chaos and slaughter. The fate of the battle was uncertain, with each side momentarily gaining the upper hand only to face stiffened resolve from the other. It soon became apparent to both sides that the American cannon would decide the battle. American cannister devastated Santa Anna's lines. And when Taylor ordered double cannister, even more devastation followed. Santa Anna became determined to take the cannons at all costs.

Late that afternoon, as the fight raged around the U.S. cannons and the battle was still very much touch and go, with both sides nearing exhaustion, Davis's First Mississippi stormed into action, stemming the Mexican advance and turning the tide of the battle—again.

Both armies, seemingly by mutually exhausted consent, ceased fighting almost as soon as night fell.

In the morning, Santa Anna was gone. Hoping to annihilate Taylor's relatively small army, he instead left most of northern Mexico in American hands. Buena Vista was a disastrous defeat for Mexico, a narrow escape for the United States and a life-changing victory for Jefferson Davis.

Brierfield

1847–1861

Back home, the wounded war hero set about fulfilling the promise he had made to his wife: a home of her own.

The land had been successful. Jefferson's trusted enslaved man and overseer, James Pemberton, had seen to that. So had his wife, Varina. She was determined for Brierfield to succeed entirely independently of her brother-in-law. She pored over plantation matters, reflecting along the way, "I have become quite a savage, I declare, I feel better alone than with anyone, though my own plate looks very lonely, and I tear my food in silence."[116] When Davis returned from Mexico, the flourishing land was ready for a house, a home.

Brierfield would be Jefferson and Varina's home. *Their* home. It would imitate elements of the homes of Varina's parents, Hurricane Plantation and the standard home of a planter of the Deep South, with its concomitant fields, space and Greek columns. And yet, it would be designed to their specifications. It would suit their land and personalities.

Remembering the destruction wrought by the storm of 1824 on Hurricane Plantation, considering that Brierfield sat beyond the pale of frequent social gatherings and taking into account the geography of the land, Jefferson and Varina settled on a one-story home with massive porches on the front and back, with smaller porches accessible from each of the bedrooms.[117] (As an added benefit, Jefferson, still on crutches from his wound in Mexico, would not have to navigate stairs.)[118] The house was painted white with dark green window shutters.[119]

With Varina's enthusiastic approval, Jefferson insisted on well-manicured flower gardens, especially those with roses. Varina later recalled: "My husband was very fond of cultivating trees and of seeing roses and ornamental shrubs blooming about us. We worked together in the garden the greater part of the day."[120]

When the couple wasn't gardening together, they enjoyed riding their horses together. Varina wrote of their "daily ride on our fastest horses, with races on the smooth road wherever we found one….There was thirty seconds' difference in the speed of our horses, our races were rather even, and we enjoyed the exercise exceedingly. Nothing could be more pleasant than the dense shade through which we could ride for miles, in air redolent of the perfume of the moss, flowers, wild crabapple and plum blossoms."[121]

Only one situation threatened the couple's domestic tranquility. In 1844, Joseph and Jefferson's brother-in-law Judge David Bradford was murdered outside the Washington, Mississippi courthouse by a disgruntled litigant. Joseph welcomed his sister and her seven children into Hurricane. The family of eight would make frequent trips to visit Varina at her house. (The visits were reciprocated as infrequently as possible by Varina.) The new homeowner dreaded seeing the brood of Bradfords arrive, as the children were wild and unruly and destructive to her new house, especially her carpets, which tended to be stained with food and drink whenever the hellions left.

It was after one such visit that Joseph proposed a plan to Jefferson. Why not extend Brierfield so that the house could accommodate their sister Amanda and her seven children? Jefferson and Varina could live on one side, the Bradfords on the other. Needless to say, Varina was incensed at the proposal. A cold war between Hurricane and Brierfield erupted, with Jefferson stuck in the middle.

In the end, Varina emerged triumphant. She later explained, "Mrs. Bradford and I mutually declined to live together, neither of us willing to be subordinate in household jurisdiction, which resulted in Mr. Davis and my taking possession of our house alone."[122]

The next decade passed peaceably for the couple. No doubt, the distance between Joseph and Varina caused by Jefferson's frequent political appointments to Washington, D.C., helped. But in 1859, tensions once again flared. Varina gave birth to her fourth child, a baby boy. She wanted to name the child after her father, but Jefferson insisted he be named Joseph in honor of his brother. Varina was aghast and wrote home to her mother, "I could never participate in paying, in my opinion, the highest compliment in a woman's power to a man whose very name was only suggestive to me of injustice and unkindness from my youth up to middle age….I don't abuse Jeff's brother, but I came so close to hating him."[123]

This time, Jefferson got his way, and the boy was christened Joseph Evan Davis.

Two years later, the civil war at Davis Bend was usurped by another civil war on a far grander scale. The fight between Varina and Joseph for the possession and affection of Jefferson Davis's heart would recede deep into the background as cataclysmic events upended the lives of all at Hurricane and Brierfield Plantations.

CIVIL WAR

1861–1865

When Mississippi seceded from the Union on January 9, 1861, Jefferson Davis called it the "saddest day of my life." He remained in Congress another twelve days until official word reached him of his state's break with his country, and then he resigned his post as a United States senator and returned to Mississippi.[124]

Fearing that war was inevitable, he nevertheless hoped it could be avoided. Always realistic, he accepted a commission as major general of Mississippi's armed forces. Determined to return to his home in the event that war did, in fact, erupt, he took his wife and his three children to Brierfield on February 1, 1861.[125] He wrote to a friend in Washington, D.C., "I found much to be done and have entered upon to me the most agreeable of all labors planting shrubs and trees and directing the operations of my field…ploughing and cleaning up for another crop."[126]

Meanwhile, on February 4, a convention of secessionists was convened in Montgomery, Alabama. The new Confederate States were in the middle of electing their first president. Five days later, the vote went to the states. Jefferson Davis's name was at the top of the ballot. Initially, Georgia was divided, and South Carolina worried about Davis's conservativism. All the other seceding states wanted Davis. Virginia, which had not yet seceded, quietly pushed for the experienced and politically savvy Davis as well. When the final vote was tabulated half an hour later, Jefferson Davis was the unanimous choice as the first president of the Confederate States of America.[127]

Jefferson Davis, photographed in his later years. *Library of Congress.*

A dispatch rider arrived at Davis Bend late in the afternoon. He found Davis outside with Varina, helping with rose cuttings. He handed the former senator the telegram informing him that he had been elected president of the Confederate States of America. Varina would later recall the fateful note that irrevocably changed both their lives. She said her husband looked so pained that she feared a terrible catastrophe had befallen a family member. "After a few minutes' painful silence," he shared the contents of the telegram "as a man might speak of a sentence of death."[128]

Two days later, Davis's enslaved workers rowed him out to the Mississippi River, where he boarded a steamboat headed for Vicksburg. There, he was greeted with cheers, parades and adulation. Within a week, he was inaugurated the first and only president of the Confederate States of America.

Jefferson Davis would not see Brierfield or Vicksburg for seven long years.

EPILOGUE

In 1888, Jefferson Davis gave his last public address to a group of young men in Mississippi City.[129]

> [My political beliefs lay] *buried in the grave of the Confederacy.… Men in whose hands the destinies of our Southland lies…the past is dead. Let it bury its dead, its hopes and aspirations; before you lies the future—a future full of golden promise; a future of expanding national glory, before which all the world shall stand amazed.…Let me beseech you to lay aside all rancor, all bitter sectional feelings, and to make your places in the ranks of those who will bring about a consummation devoutly to be wished—a reunited country.*[130]

On November 6, 1889, Davis boarded a steamboat for his annual trip back to his treasured Brierfield. On board, he became so sick that the captain sailed right past Davis's home and left him in the hands of a doctor in Vicksburg. As soon as he could, Davis boarded a boat to Brierfield and took to bed, refusing to summon a doctor. Instead, he wrote his final letter to Varina, a note advising her that he would be returning home immediately. The letter was written in the hand of a seriously ill man, barely legible and vague: "Lest you should hear alarming write say I have suffered much but by the help of the Lord."[131]

The next day, he wrote his final lines when his overseer's young daughter asked for his autograph in her memory book. Davis scrawled his name and the message, "May all your paths be peaceful and pleasant, charged with the best fruit, the doing good to others."[132]

Varina had already learned the day before via telegram that her husband of almost forty-five years was fading fast. Two days later, she was headed toward Brierfield on a steamboat—the same day Davis was headed south. The two vessels met midriver, and Varina moved to her husband's cabin. The couple landed in New Orleans, and for the next three weeks, Varina rarely left her husband's side as his condition vacillated between stable and improving. Suddenly, on December 5, 1889, chills seized Jefferson, and he lapsed into unconsciousness. As always, Varina stayed by his side, holding his hand until there was no longer any pulse.

Jefferson Davis, American, war hero, slaveowner, farmer, secessionist and unrepented rebel, died just after midnight on December 6, 1889.[133]

Varina's story would continue another seventeen years—far from her and Jefferson's beloved Brierfield.

7

SISTER MARY IGNATIUS SUMNER
AND THE SISTERS OF MERCY

1860–1895

My God,
I am yours for time and eternity,
Lord, I am yours forever.
It is you who must teach me to trust in your Providence, Loving Lord.

You are a God of love and tenderness.
I place my trust in you,
And I ask that you grant me acceptance of your will,
Loving Lord.

Refrain:
Take from my heart all painful anxiety.
Let nothing sadden me but sin.
And then let my delight be hoping to see your face,
God, my all.

—Suscipe of Catherine McAuley[134]

Sister Ignatius Sumner was dying. Having nursed countless patients to health and death, she knew the end was near. Scenes from her seventy years of living rushed through her mind. A teacher at heart, a nurse of the body and soul by necessity, Sister Ignatius had always had a fascination with history. She, like every other human person, had lived it. Yet she had lived through an unusually eventful and traumatic era of American history. She wanted it recorded. The story of her and her sisters must be recorded for posterity. The world needs its Peters, Andrews and Judes; it also needs its Matthews, Marks and Lukes.

When not engaged in her teaching and nursing duties, Sister Ignatius began to compile a "register of events" that morphed into a part memoir, part history of the lives of her and her fellow Sisters, with a particular emphasis on the Civil War, the yellow fever epidemics and St. Francis Xavier Academy.

Before she died, Sister Ignatius urged her friend and coworker in the vineyard Sister Mary DeSales Browne, "Please keep these manuscripts for us after you have finished with them, as all the latter part is from memory, and we have no other Record than this, which may be interesting to our Sisters at some future time if preserved."[135]

Sister DeSales honored Sister Ignatius's request, and the story of the Sisters of Mercy in Mississippi was preserved.

❧

1895

With Sister Ignatius's end approaching, her contemplative life gave her plenty of opportunity for reflection. So many scenes, those lived by her and those related to her by her companions, brought back vivid memories. She would have recalled the dangerous times of the great war and epidemics; the good times with her Sisters; the baptisms, first communions, confirmations, graduations, marriages and taking of religious vows; laughter and joy that came with being so intimately connected with a community; and, most importantly, the people she met, mostly her students and patients. After all, human souls, her own and others', were the reason she took her vows and faithfully served others as a Sister of Mercy for more than half a century.

❧

1865

Sister Ignatius must have taken some satisfaction in a life well lived. Two men at the highest stages of government—rival presidents—had heaped public praise upon her and her fellow Sisters of Mercy in Mississippi and beyond.

After the Vicksburg Campaign, General Grant, the conqueror of Vicksburg, described to President Abraham Lincoln a wartime scene in Vicksburg in which a Sister of Mercy had nursed a dying soldier. The scene had left a permanent mark on Grant's psyche. Lincoln responded that he had seen the same nurses performing similar feats in Washington. Soon after, he ordered the White House painter, Florence Meyer, to preserve the scene on canvas for posterity.[136]

President Lincoln proclaimed, "Of all the forms of charity and benevolence seen in the crowded wards of hospitals, those of the Catholic sisters were among the most efficient....As they went from cot to cot distributing the medicines prescribed, or administering the cooling, strengthening draughts as directed, they were veritable angels of mercy."[137]

The Sisters of Mercy, depicted on a waterfront mural in Vicksburg. *Ryan Starrett.*

On the defeated side, President Jefferson Davis joined his Northern nemeses in praise of the same Sisters: "I can never forget your kindness to the sick and wounded during our darkest days. And I know not how to testify my gratitude and respect for every member of your noble order."[138]

✺

1895

The scenes that prompted such gratitude from two divergent and powerful men drifted through Sister Ignatius's mind as she made notes in her "register of events" and reminisced as her end approached.

✺

1860–1865

On October 9, 1860, exactly two months before Mississippi seceded from the Union, Father Francis Xavier Leray boarded a train for Vicksburg. With him went four Sisters of Mercy and two aspiring postulants. Among them was a nervous but eager Sister Ignatius Sumner. A close relation of the despised abolitionist Charles Sumner of Massachusetts, Sister Ignatius would now make her home among rabid secessionists. With her rode the first sisters of the Mississippi mission: Sisters Mary DeSales Browne, Mary Vincent Browne and Stephana Warde.

A week later, the Sisters arrived at their convent on Crawford Street. Four days later, they dedicated their new home to Saint Catherine of Siena. Unknown to them at the time, the Sisters would need all the intercession they could get from the fiery fourteenth-century nun who lived an exemplary life of personal holiness but was not afraid to boss rulers and popes around. Only strong-willed nuns in the spirit of their patroness would survive in patriarchal, anti-Catholic Mississippi.

Just two weeks after arriving in Vicksburg, Sister Ignatius stood before her first students. St. Francis Xavier Academy had an inaugural enrollment of 60 students. By the start of the 1861 school year, enrollment had more than doubled to 142 students. (The Sisters' Sunday school program also taught 78 boys, 121 girls and 25 Black students.)[139]

No doubt, the Sisters were off to a successful start. They had begun planting the seeds of their faith on fertile ground. But then disaster struck. Just nineteen months after opening their doors, those same doors closed when it became apparent that the federal troops who had bombarded Vicksburg in May 1862, intended to stay until the "Gibraltar of the Confederacy" was in Yankee hands.

When the Cook family invited the Sisters to stay at their plantation safely outside of town, six of the Sisters gratefully accepted and began moving their chapel furniture to the plantation. There, they set up an impromptu school for the Cook's Black enslaved children and a number of enslaved people from neighboring plantations. Four other Sisters remained behind in Vicksburg to nurse the sick who had been brought to their convent turned hospital. The situation quickly deteriorated, however, due to a constant barrage of federal cannonballs lobbed into the city. Two columns were obliterated, and a cannonball was fired into an upstairs room. For the safety of all, a new hospital was established in Mississippi Springs, thirty miles east of Vicksburg. The four Sisters continued their nursing duties there.[140]

The Sisters move to the Cook plantation, and Mississippi Springs was a terrifying introduction to the next two years of their collective lives. The order would move farther east to Jackson and then north to Oxford and Corinth, back to Jackson and farther south to Shelby Springs. They lived sub specie aeternitatis, or "under the shadow of eternity," for much of the duration of the war. Their homes and hospitals were struck by cannonballs, they faced constant exposure to infection and disease, the interminable hours, hunger, stress, lack of sleep, depression and death.

Finally, on May 23, 1864, Bishop Elder asked the Sisters to return to their convent in Vicksburg. The city was firmly in federal hands, as was much of Mississippi. The war dragged on, but the outcome was becoming increasingly clear. The Sisters would be needed if Vicksburg was to be rebuilt beneath the Stars and Stripes. Five days later, the Sisters of Mercy were back in Vicksburg.

After a bitter but ultimately successful battle to get their convent back, the Sisters reopened their school. The immediate enrollment of two hundred students demonstrated just how badly the residents of Vicksburg wanted to return to a sense of normalcy. An additional two hundred attended Catechism classes on Sunday.[141] With only four Sisters having returned—the other five remained behind as nurses in Shelby Springs—the

The Sisters of Mercy Convent in Vicksburg (1860). *Catholic Diocese of Jackson, Mississippi.*

workload was overwhelming. (Sister DeSales added "cook" to her already extensive résumé.)[142]

A year after the Sisters' return to Vicksburg, the war finally ended, and the Sisters reunited. Their convent was returned, and their school—their original raison d'etre—reopened. Routine had returned to the war-weary Sisters, but the scars of the war were permanent.

As Sister Ignatius's end approached, so many horrid memories must have returned to her aging but still sharp mind.

The Yankee prisoner did not have long to live. Fluid filled his lungs, and pneumonia would soon put an end to his suffering. The dying soldier told one of the Sisters that he would very much like to see his companions one last time before he died. She immediately asked the prison guard if his request was feasible.

When the sun began to set, a Confederate guard led a handful of blue-coated prisoners into the hospital. Sister asked the pneumoniac if he recognized any of them. The man's face lit up, and he shook each of his comrades' hands, addressing them by name, for the final time. After crying out, "Where are you? I cannot see!" he passed away.

His companions were promptly led back to prison.[143]

She remembered the soldier from Tennessee, lying wounded in the Jackson, Mississippi hospital. An artery in his neck had been severed, making it necessary to plug the gash with a thumb. When one off the Sisters came to him, he refused her administrations, claiming that he would not be touched by a Catholic.

Eventually, out of necessity, he yielded, and one of the Sisters placed her thumb in his wound. Henceforward, he was never comfortable unless one of the Sisters was nearby.[144]

Sister Ignatius would have recalled the train ride from the Sisters' hospital in Selma, when the train went off its tracks. She and Sister DeSales were returning to Vicksburg at Bishop Elder's request when the train flipped over three miles outside Meridian. Their own car was saved by a tree trunk and held upright, albeit at an angle. Beneath them lay a deep, dark pool of muddy water. That night, the Sisters slept in the car, guarding their luggage.[145]

YELLOW FEVER

1878

Being a river town, Vicksburg had always been susceptible to the diseases that accompanied trade. Being nurses during America's deadliest war to date, Sister Ignatius and her fellow Sisters of Mercy had plenty of experience with a plethora of illnesses: malaria, pneumonia, dysentery, anemia, asthma, erysipelas, gonorrhea, hepatitis, jaundice, meningitis and syphilis.[146]

But the deadliest of all—yellow fever—tore through Vicksburg and its environs with deadly efficiency, most notably in 1878.

Sister DeSales wrote to Sister Austin Carroll of New Orleans:

> *The fever here is of the worst character I have ever seen. Deaths frequently occur within a few hours. Whole families have been swept away. There is scarcely an Italian left in the city. We found a dead body in every house on the levee. The City Hospital has been turned over to us, and our Sisters from our other houses have come here to aid us. The whole place is a desert. Not a human being to be seen in the streets, save the black-robed Sisters hurrying on their mission of mercy, or some member of the benevolent societies. From*

Bishop William Henry Elder. *Catholic Diocese of Jackson, Mississippi.*

morning till night, good Bishop Elder is to be found at the bedside of the dying, administering the Sacraments, consoling and encouraging all. If he gives himself any rest these days, no one knows when. Pray God to come to our aid. He alone can help us now.[147]

The ghosts of Sister Ignatius's patients would have haunted her during her quiet hours.

There was the man who spoke to the priest visiting him: "Father, I have waited for a message from the Master for five years, and this is what he has sent me. My family starving and in rags and I about to leave them. I want nothing to do with him." The priest confided in one of the Sisters what the dying man had told him. The next time the priest came to the fading man's house, he found him in bed, clutching a crucifix. The house was clean, food was in the cupboard, and his family wore new(er) clothing. The dying but grateful man spoke: "Now indeed, Father, I know how good God is and that he has not forsaken me."

Shortly after, the man died, but not before the Sisters promised to look after his family. The Sisters looked after his wife and children until enough donations from the North allowed the family to return to their roots in Massachusetts.[148]

And then there were the spirits who remained elusive—"the empty chairs at empty tables."[149] And the empty desks.

> *Our school was opened in the middle of November. The fever had been particularly destructive to little children, as in almost every case it was combined with meningitis; and when the Sisters who had the infant school room went in that morning and missed thirty little familiar faces, she could not conceal her emotion, but wept over the lost, but now happy little cherubs. Nothing could have been a sadder or more striking contrast during the fever than the cloudless blue of the heavens; the softness of the air and the beauty of the nights, the moon looking down like the Angel of Justice, so lustrous, yet so coldly, upon the City of the dead. Houses closed, stores vacated, and often, except ourselves and the Physicians, scarcely a creature was to be seen, the inhabitants consisting of two classes, nurses and sick.*[150]

No doubt, Sister Ignatius harkened back to the horrible toll of the epidemic, which she had recorded in her "register of events":

> *The assistant priests, Father Oberfield and Father Huber, were next down with the fever; six priests were already dead and about twenty Religious of various Orders in the Diocese. Six Nazareth Sisters of Charity had died in Holly Springs, one of them offering her life for the Bishop's preservation, two also were dead at Yazoo City and the rest ill when two of her Sisters, one of them just recovered from the fever, went up to nurse them. They*

Sister Verona, a Sister of Mercy, photographed during the Civil War by Mathew Brady. *U.S. National Archives.*

succeeded in saving the lives of the rest, except the Superior, Sister M. Lawrence, who was beginning to convalesce, when Rev. J.B. Mouton, their pastor who had been a most zealous and self-sacrificing laborer amidst all the deprivations of an extensive country Mission, was taken with the fever, and died in a short time, his constitution having been already exhausted. Sister M. Lawrence seemed to receive a shock by the news, and died a few days after.[151]

The yellow fever proved to be as destructive to Vicksburg as had been General Grant's siege. Sister Ignatius recorded in her register of events: "The deaths were variously estimated from 1,300 to 1,500, but we believe them nearer 2,000, as many were buried at a time, and many in the country not in the Sexton's report."[152] (Vicksburg had 4,000 residents at the time.)[153]

THE OTHER YEARS

The Civil War and yellow fever epidemics were the most dramatic times of Sister Ignatius's life, yet they were not necessarily the most important. The majority of her working life consisted of performing mundane tasks: washing dishes, sweeping the convent floors, preparing for next day's classes, holding detentions, laundering habits, teaching catechism on Sundays.

All those tasks, performed diligently and with love, led to the formation of countless relationships, which sustained and strengthened Sister Ignatius during her half-century of service—and now, as she approached the end of her vocation.

The relationships she had with soldiers and patients she nursed were most often transitory. The patients either recovered and returned home or died. Most of her students, however, grew into functioning members of her Vicksburg community.

Many of them remained permanently in her life.

Ten-year-old John Kearney was chosen to welcome the new Sisters to their convent. Despite being from a Catholic family with twelve children from Baltimore, young John had never seen a Sister before. He was nervous.

He left the basket of supplies by the convent door, knocked and then took off to the street. A surprised Sister answered the door and saw the supplies—and then the shy boy off in the distance. The conversation that ensued turned young John Kearney into a devoted acolyte of the Sisters. He would bring them supplies, help with household chores, drive them about during the Civil War, smuggle them into quarantined cities during the epidemics and carry their coffins from church to cemetery.[154]

Sister Ignatius recalled that after the war, there were so, so many destitute. The school was filled with pupils looking for learning, comfort and normalcy.

And it wasn't just the children who sought learning from the Sisters. Adults, too, looked to better their conditions through education. The Sisters began to teach night school. One of their most colorful pupils was John Loviza, a riverboat captain who had yet to live down an incident when, as a younger man, he had wrecked his tugboat at the end of Clay Street. A humbled John became one of the Sisters' first night students. Many years later, he wrote, "Among those who taught me at night school

Sister Jachim, photographed during the Civil War by Mathew Brady. *U.S. National Archives.*

were Sister Antonia, Sister Philomena and Sister Xavier and I feel sure that they are all in heaven for they surely were good to me."[155]

Neither would Sister Ignatius ever forget those she was most intimate with: the band of Sisters who had devoted their lives to living in community and serving the less fortunate.

She remembered the leader of the Vicksburg Sisters, Mary DeSales Browne. Trained as a surgical nurse in Pittsburgh, Sister DeSales suffered a health scare in 1859 and recuperated near her order's school in Baltimore.

In 1860, Bishop William Henry Elder, Diocese of Natchez, Mississippi, requested a handful of Sister-teachers from his home diocese of Baltimore. Sister DeSales was chosen to lead the sisterhood one thousand miles south to form a school in the heart of what was then close to the frontier.

Upon learning of her assignment to Vicksburg, Sister DeSales accepted her death sentence:

> *I tried to remain perfectly resigned to God's Will, in spite of the feeling that with my ill health I was unfit to establish our order so far away; but the thought that I would have to bear this cross for only a short time, since my frail body indicated a journey to heaven rather than to Mississippi, I calmly awaited until the burden of administration would be laid on abler shoulders.*[156]

Despite her prognostications of doom, Sister DeSales would lead the Mississippi mission for half a century, until her death in 1910.

Her life paralleled that of Sister Ignatius.

During the war, late at night, Sister DeSales went outside the camp and chopped wood so that the wounded soldiers might at least suffer in warmth and light. "She set the example of service, compassion, and Christian love."[157] Sister DeSales would continue to set an example for her charges in the community, the classroom and the hospital for another half-century.

HUMOR

If "humor is the most infallible sign of the presence of God,"[158] then Sister Ignatius was closer to God than most. Despite living and serving the destitute and dying—situations that would have depressed most and broken many—Sister Ignatius was able to find levity amid hardship and suffering. No doubt, these memories helped ease her challenging odyssey through life.

While Sister Ignatius was working in the hospital at Mississippi Springs, the town began to send food to the invalids.[159] And it was the beauties of the town who brought the sustenance to the wounded. Some of the male nurses, upon seeing the approach of the belles, would leap onto a cot, shoes and all, hoping to receive some kind words and ministrations from the young ladies.[160]

Sister Ignatius recalled her fellow Sister who was asked to take charge of the baking but found herself totally inadequate to the calling. Panicked, she placed a statue of the Virgin Mary in the back of the oven. Afterward, her baking was deemed acceptable.[161]

While the federals were bombarding Jackson, one of the shells passed through the ward filled with the wounded and exploded in the chicken coop. Standing nearby, the terrified and plump cook took what cover she could, placing her head beneath the steps. The rest of her would not fit, and her posterior remained exposed. Seeing an opportunity to avenge an earlier wrong, the cook's sister snatched a fork and poked her sister's ample buttocks.[162]

ᴓ

DECEMBER 12, 1881

As a foretaste of the praise that would be heaped on herself—if not immediately upon her death, by posterity and in the next world—Sister Ignatius was no doubt pleased and humbled by the words of Father Picherit at her order's fiftieth jubilee.

> *The valiant men ceased, and rested in Israel; until Debora arose, a Mother arose in Israel. There was not a shield on Israel and the spear lay broken on the ground.* [Judges 5:7]

The founder of the Sisters of Mercy, Mother Catherine McCauley, had been caste in the image of the Hebrew heroines. She was born in turbulent times, lived in turbulent times and died in turbulent times. Her Daughters/Sisters in America flourished, suffered and endured. Their mission, the mission of the great commission, to spread the Gospel to all peoples, would continue. Father Picherit concluded his homily: "I do homage to their deeds, and salute their virtues."[163]

ᴓ

SIENA, ITALY

Four Hundred Years Previous, 1380

[Of Catherine of Siena:] *Her own task was clearly marked within a plan so great that she could see only a tiny part of it, and that stretched across the centuries and the destinies of hosts of men and women. There were saints and popes and bishops, monks and nuns and kings and others, and often the greatest warriors were very simple people, children and cripples and very young girls, people enduring rather than acting.*[164]

∞

IRELAND

Forty Years Previous, 1841

Mother Catherine McCauley, foundress of the Sisters of Mercy, the spiritual descendant of Catherine of Siena, the hopeful coresident of her namesake, lay on her deathbed. She instructed her fellow Sisters "to be sure that all the Sisters are given a comfortable cup of tea when I am gone."

∞

JERUSALEM

1,850 Years Previous, 30 CE

"For I was hungry and you gave me food, I was thirsty and you gave me drink, a stranger and you welcomed me, naked and you clothed me, ill and you cared for me, in prison and you visited me."

Then the righteous will answer him and say, "Lord, when did we see you hungry and feed you, or thirsty and give you drink? When did we see you a stranger and welcome you, or naked and clothe you? When did we see you ill or in prison, and visit you?"

And the king will say to them in reply, "Amen, I say to you, whatever you did for one of the least brothers of mine, you did for me."[165]

VICKSBURG

1895

Sister Ignatius's eyes began to dim. Soon, they would fail her. But her spirit and sense of service went on. Sister Ignatius continued to teach her students by day and another batch at night. Her mind was so sharp, she was able to teach reading, history and math right up until malaria claimed her earthly life.[166]

But her work lives on, not only in her "register of events," but also in the long, uninterrupted line of her spiritual progeny who continue her mission to serve society's least fortunate. It's the same long, uninterrupted line that Sister Ignatius herself had been a part of—the thread of history linking all persons of goodwill.

RICOCHET

Act Like a Man, Die Like a Fool

OCTOBER 15, 1890

It was almost midnight, and New Orleans's superintendent of police, David Hennessy, was making his way home through the rain. He was heading for the little cottage on Girod Street that he shared with his mother. He would have to avoid Basin Street, his normal route. New Orleans's unpaved streets turned into a muddy mess when it rained. Basin Street was particularly treacherous.

Hennessy walked that night with a cop friend, Billy O'Connor. They decided to stop in at Dominic Virget's saloon for a snack of a dozen oysters and milk. Hennessy's father had been a drunk, murdered in a bar. Hennessy didn't touch alcohol. But he loved milk.

Hennessy and O'Connor sat there talking while they ate—two Irishmen and New Orleanians through and through. Hennessy was thirty-two years old, with a strong chin, grand mustache and lean body. He didn't drink or gamble, but he was as tough as anyone. He'd proven it when he captured the Sicillian bandit Giuseppe Esposito nine years earlier. The bandit had been hiding out in New Orleans—Hennessy sent him back across the sea. And he'd proven it when he executed another cop, Thomas Devereaux, three months later. He put a pistol to the back of his head and pulled the trigger. Devereaux had threatened Hennessy's cousin—with words and with his pistol. In those days, honor was defended with guns.

Hennessy had been tried for murder. He had been acquitted after a long jury deliberation. He thought his career as a cop was over. But the mayor

DAVID C. HENNESSY, LATE CHIEF OF POLICE.

New Orleans Superintendent of Police David Hennessy, as depicted in *Harper's Weekly* (1891). *HathiTrust.*

had brought him back seven years later and offered him the superintendent job.

Hennessy was tasked with cleaning up a police force that had grown notoriously corrupt. The ranks of the force had been filled with "deadhead" special officers, appointed by the previous city administration to act as a private political army. Cops were shaking down local business owners. Public shootouts were frequent. And good cops were being paid less because so much money was flowing to the deadheads.

Hennessy got rid of the deadheads and began cracking down on crime in the city, particularly illegal gambling. His force made more than twenty thousand arrests in his first year as superintendent. But there was one problem that Hennessy couldn't seem to solve: the Sicilians who had begun immigrating to New Orleans in the 1880s (and who would eventually arrive by the hundreds of thousands) were feuding.

Much of the tension stemmed from the fruit-unloading business on the New Orleans waterfront. Central American bananas, coconuts, pineapples, limes and mangoes had begun arriving at the port by the shipload. The Provenzano family possessed the contract for unloading the fruit—until the contract was given to the Matrangas and Locasios. Hennessy had tried to mediate between the two groups, but his efforts were unsuccessful.

In May 1890, Tony Matranga and some of his workers were ambushed by shotgun-wielding assailants hiding in the brush. One minute, they'd been riding in a wagon, laughing and talking after a long day of work. The next minute, pandemonium. A slug blew Matranga's knee apart. He lost his leg. Other ambush-style shootings followed. Hennessy was intent on stopping the violence—and punishing those responsible.

After their meal, Hennessy and O'Connor continued on to Girod Street. O'Connor bid his friend farewell and continued walking toward the river. Hennessy walked the short distance to his house, reached his front door and began digging in his pocket for his key. He squinted to see by the light of a low-hanging electric streetlight that was near the end of its life.

Hennessy, too, was near the end of his life. The weapon of choice in "vendetta" murders, as the press had dubbed them, was the shotgun.

Assassins waited for their victims and sprayed them with buckshot before they even knew what was happening. Assassins were waiting for Hennessy the night of October 15. A crack sounded, and Hennessy's body was riddled with shot. A slug passed through both his lungs as he stood on his front doorstep. One shotgun blast—and then another.

The lawman pulled his service revolver and returned fire. The ambushers got away. He stumbled down the street, where he was met by O'Connor. O'Connor had been so close to his friend during the shooting that he saw the muzzle blasts. "Oh, Billy," Hennessy moaned.

O'Connor asked who had done it. Hennessy answered with one word: "Dagoes."

He lived another few hours, dying in an opiate-induced sleep the following morning. New Orleans exploded with rage. The city was in a bloody mood, and the press stoked the bloodlust every step of the way. The assassination of Hennessy would lead to one of the worst lynchings in American history. And the fallout from the assassination would eventually make its way to Vicksburg, where two newspaper editors would mimic the New Orleans–style violence. One of the editors would try to live up to the violent ideal his peers had promoted before and after the lynching—to "act like a man." But in the end, he would give only his blood to the street.[167]

The story of David Hennessy's assassination reached the public in vivid detail, because the New Orleans press reported on it—and on other Italian-related crimes—with great enthusiasm. It was journalists who described the ambush of Matranga and his men not simply as a vendetta, but as *the* vendetta. The substitution of *the* for *a* turned *vendetta* into a cultural institution brought over from the old world rather than a simple isolated act of revenge.

"It seems the 'vendetta' has been imported to New Orleans along with the Italians, Corsicans, and Sicilians," the *Lafayette Advertiser* wrote following the ambush. The trial of the men arrested for the Matranga shooting came to be known in papers as the "Vendetta Case."[168]

In the wake of Hennessy's murder, Mayor Joseph Shakespeare announced that Hennessy had been murdered by the "mafia"—a concept that had germinated recently in Sicily and was foreign to Americans at the time. The press ran with the exotic concept, repeating the "mafia" theme and creating the sense among readers that New Orleans was being influenced by

ANTONIO SCAFFIDI.   JOSEPH P. MACHECA.   A. BAGNETTO.   JOHN MATRANGA.   PIETRO MASTERO.

SUPPOSED LEADERS AND INSTRUMENTS OF "THE MAFIA."

Some of the Italian men accused of being mafia members in the wake of David Hennessy's assassination. The sketch originally appeared in *Harper's Weekly* (1891). *HathiTrust.*

a secretive, powerful Sicilian crime syndicate. The press began connecting nearly every crime involving Italians to the mafia, with little evidence.

The Washington Post joined in, summarizing the mafia in New Orleans thusly:

> *Over the city of New Orleans hung a vague pall; in its midst was a secret society which had no visible existence, yet was perfectly organized; whose membership was of wide extent, yet which never met twice in the same place; a society whose speech was foreign and strange, and to whom assassination was not unknown, was indeed, its weapon of defense, if not the source of its power. This society had permeated the arteries of trade, had entered the courts of justice, had struck terror in every heart, had slain the only man who dared defy it.*[169]

Anti-Italian sentiment grew. Shakespeare's announcement was probably politically motivated—Italians in New Orleans generally supported his political rivals. In reality, the mafia in New Orleans was more a compelling story than an actual organized crime ring.[170]

The press did not stop at asserting that the Mafia was rife in New Orleans. Reporters actively participated in criminal investigations. The morning after Hennessy's assassination, one of Hennessy's neighbors, a cobbler and recent immigrant from Sicily named Pietro Monasterio, stood outside with the rest of the neighborhood, trying to learn what had happened. But unlike most, Monasterio wore clean shoes. Police searched the shack he lived in and found a pair of muddy shoes under his bed. A reporter took a long piece of paper and pressed it into a footprint in the street, and then he compared the paper to Monasterio's shoes. The reporter said the outline was a perfect match. Monasterio was beaten badly and arrested.[171]

Monasterio's arrest kicked off the mass arrest of Italians in New Orleans. In all, more than one hundred were arrested. A few weeks later, a grand jury indicted nineteen of them for Hennessy's murder. The *Times-Democrat* began running large sketches of the accused on its front page.

The following spring, the men were tried. The first nine defendants were either acquitted or given mistrials due to a lack of evidence. Eight members of the mayor's "Committee of Fifty," which had been convened to investigate the Hennessy murder, gathered that night to discuss what must be done to right the injustice of the undesired verdicts. The next morning, a notice appeared on the front page of the *Times-Democrat*, with terse instructions: "All good citizens are invited to attend a mass meeting on Saturday, March 14, at 10 o'clock a.m. at Clay Statue, to take steps to remedy the failure of justice in the Hennessy case. Come prepared for action."[172]

It was a thinly veiled call for mob violence. More than ten thousand citizens subsequently gathered at the Henry Clay statue on Canal Street to listen to elites, including the mayor's campaign manager, William S. Parkerson, incite them. "The jury has failed," Parkerson said. "Now the people have to act."

Parkerson, planter James Houston and newspaper editor John Wickliffe then led a posse of sixty armed men into the prison and shot to death eleven Italians. Two of the men's bodies were strung up outside the prison to the cheers of the mob. Parkerson announced, "You have acted like men—now, go home like men."[173]

The next day, the *Times-Democrat*, which had been complicit in organizing the lynch mob, published a story that took up more than two full broadsheet pages. Headlined "Avenged," the story recounted the violence in stomach-turning detail and included sketches of the lynched men's faces, a sketch of the prison surrounded by the mob of thousands and a sketch of the lynched men's bodies laid out on the prison floor. The story described the lynched men as "assassins" and said the lynch mob was quiet, calm and orderly. "They were still grim and silent, but they walked rapidly along, having determination fixedly stamped on every feature."

The *New Democrat* reported on the lynching with gleeful support, using the "avenged" language and writing that "eleven Italians pay the penalty of their crimes."

The *Daily Picayune* characterized the lynching as the righting of a great wrong: "Yesterday the people of this city rose in wrath and indignation at the corruption and perversion of the machinery which was delegated the administration of justice.…They took in their hand the sword of justice,

An 1891 photograph of Canal Street, the "broadest street in the world." *Library of Congress.*

and they did not lay it down until they had executed vengeance upon the criminals whom the corrupt ministers of justice had excused and set free."

The New Orleans papers were caught up in—and stoking—the bloodlust. But in Vicksburg, an editor stood up for the rule of law.

On March 16, two days after the lynching, readers in Vicksburg opened the *Evening Post* to read two editorials by publisher John G. Cashman. One had been written before the lynchings, and the other had been written after.

In his first editorial, written after the publication of the New Orleans call to action but before news of the lynching had reached Vicksburg, Cashman urged New Orleanians to think carefully about what they wanted to do—to describe how, exactly, justice had been subverted ("a well-digested and deliberately-considered statement of the evils to be remedied") and create a careful plan of action.

Cashman was clearly uneasy at the call to vigilantism, writing, "We are confident that no public violence is meant or desired by the gentlemen engaged in this movement, and we trust that they will not permit any excited appeals to the worst passions of the people."

And Cashman urged that Americans not treat Italians with prejudice. "Hennessy was doubtless murdered by Italians, but not by the Italians as a race, as a class, or for any race or national object," he wrote. "The outraged law cries out against the murderers, whoever they may be, but not against Italians."[174]

Cashman was urging restraint, deliberation, nonviolence and fairness. Perhaps the story of Vicksburg's own notorious vigilantism from more than fifty years before was on his mind.

In his second editorial, published on the front page, Cashman condemned the lynchings, reiterating that he was wholly against mob violence and racism against Italians.

"Does it not occur to the impartial mind that another great crime has been added?" Cashman wrote. "And is it not possible that in the crowd comprising the mob, there were men who take delight in the shedding of human blood, as well as men who thought they were performing a solemn duty?" Cashman wrote plainly that the mob had committed murder against defenseless prisoners and that the city was complicit by not acting to prevent the lynching.[175]

His two editorials conveyed his hope that violence would not occur—and his disappointment that it had.

On the contrary, Vicksburg's other large newspaper, the *Commercial Herald*, told citizens of Vicksburg of the lynchings with breathless enthusiasm, echoing the tone of the reporting in New Orleans. The *Herald*'s article on the lynchings, published the day after they occurred, was celebratory.

In a story headlined "Vengeance I," the *Herald* began with, "New Orleans struck Mafia a death blow today." The article justified and defended the actions of the mob, describing its actions as paradoxically "cool-headed," "quiet," "not unruly" and "determined." The mob's "work of blood" was accomplished "without unnecessary disorder, without rioting, without pillaging, and without the inflicting of suffering upon any innocent man, save one, and he was only slightly hurt." Rather than having committed a mass lynching, the men in New Orleans had done something efficient, methodical and just—for the good of the city. The article stated as fact that

Le Journaliste de l'Opposition, by C. J. Traviès. *Paris Musées*.

a "secret tribunal" had murdered Hennessy and that the trial that followed had been subverted by the mafia.[176]

Cashman's was a lone voice of restraint. And that voice was apparently infuriating to at least one other newspaperman in Vicksburg. Ernest Hardenstein was the editor of *Business*, a weekly commercial paper in the city. He was from New Orleans and had been a career newspaperman, working for multiple New Orleans papers and even serving previously as city editor for Cashman's *Post* for eighteen months.

Hardenstein used his position as editor of *Business* to criticize his former boss's position on the lynchings. He seemed particularly incensed by Cashman's charge that the lynching was racially motivated—there was no evidence to support that, Hardenstein wrote, other than the fact that all the lynched men had been Italian. And Hardenstein accused Cashman of being disingenuous: "The *Vicksburg Evening Post* waited for the expression of the *Commercial Herald* on the New Orleans uprising, and then took the other side, which view meets with universal condemnation in this city."

Hardenstein was not just criticizing Cashman's opinion; he was also accusing him of being unprofessional, of lacking the conviction of his arguments. Cashman was a petty contrarian, Hardenstein insinuated. Not a serious journalist.

Cashman responded in an editorial of his own. Cashman called *Business* a "handbill" and implied that Hardenstein was only a *self-proclaimed* editor. Hardenstein's assertion that Cashman was only writing the opposite of the *Herald* was a "willful lie," Cashman wrote. Hardenstein was the unprofessional one, Cashman implied. And on top of that, he was a damned liar.

Even though he had started the row in print, Hardenstein was enraged by the accusation of dishonesty. After reading Cashman's retort, the small, wiry thirty-five-year-old silently walked out to Washington Street, where he began pacing from storefront to storefront, person to person. He had never been called a liar before, Hardenstein told one person. He couldn't stand for it. He was going to slap Cashman, he said. He was going to "mash him in the mouth." He took off his glasses. He didn't want them damaged in the fight to come.

Hardenstein was high on reports from New Orleans of heroic men, stoic men, men acting like men, men of action. Hardenstein wanted to be a *real man*. He resolved to defend his honor with violence, as a real man should.

But he had made a tactical mistake. He had stood on Washington Street for hours, threatening Cashman, telegraphing what he planned to do. It's no surprise that Hardenstein's threats made their way to Cashman at the *Evening Post* office. Owen McQuaide, an Irishman and friend of Cashman's, had delivered the warning. He suggested maybe Cashman should take a different route home. "That will never do," Cashman said. "I have the right to go home without fear of molestation."[177]

That evening, Cashman set out for home with McQuaide. Another friend, Sam Richardson, joined him on the street. As they made their way toward Washington Street, sure enough, Hardenstein appeared, walking quickly toward Cashman. Cashman's pistol was ready. He pulled it from his pocket and fired it into Hardenstein's chest. Hardenstein stumbled and died in the Vicksburg Street. He had acted like a man—for a few hours. And he had died like a fool. Cashman, who had urged restraint, deliberation and nonviolence had struck his foe with lethal decisiveness when the moment came.

And because Hardenstein had so publicly telegraphed his intentions to do harm to Cashman, there were plenty of witnesses to testify at Cashman's murder trial. Person after person told the jury that they had heard Hardenstein's threats. Cashman was acquitted.[178]

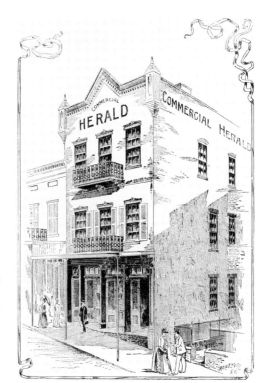

Right: The Vicksburg Herald building in 1895, originally published in *Picturesque Vicksburg*. *Library of Congress*.

Below: An advertisement for Fitzgerald's Saloon that appeared in *Picturesque Vicksburg* (1895). *Library of Congress*.

M. FITZGERALD,

Dealer in Fine Kentucky Whisky, Wines, Cigars and Tobacco.

OPPOSITE YAZOO & MISSISSIPPI VALLEY PASSENGER DEPOT.

9

Joseph Biedenharn
and the Bottling of Coca-Cola

1866–1952

Like much of the United States, Vicksburg is a land of immigrants—perhaps more so due to its position on the Mississippi River.

From Prussian Louis Ferdinand Hoffman, who migrated to Vicksburg in 1853 to successively open a hunting gun and hardware store; to Italian immigrant Alexander Brunini, whose grandson would become the Catholic bishop of the Natchez-Jackson Diocese from 1966 to 1984; the Lebanese peddlers and shop keepers, such as Gregory Thomas's grandfather who taught him, "Son, I don't care if you have to sell peanuts on the street, you work for yourself. Don't make another man rich"; the Stafinskis, Gembis, Wesoloskis, Sikorskis, Skrzypeks, Ramzas and Rapaczs of Poland who came to work the paper mills of Vicksburg; and the Irish, Chinese, Africans and Hispanics, Vicksburg has, for two hundred years, benefited from an influx of foreign immigrants, most of whom would become citizens of the United States.[179]

The Herman and Louisa Biedenharn family of Germany and Denmark were two such immigrants who left their stamp on Vicksburg.

Joe's most prized possession as a child was his little red wagon. He loved racing it up and down the street. He was often accompanied by his Danish grandfather William Lundberg. One day, his grandfather stopped Joe and asked him to look at the wagon:

> Kaere barn, *this little wagon is like many things you will build in life. The patience and care of detail used in making this wagon are more important than the little red wagon itself. Joe, anything worth building is worth building well. Plan thoughtfully, avoid mistakes, build everything on simple, substantial lines. This is the honest way of doing things, and you will find the results satisfying.*[180]

Grandfather Lundberg's advice came from an old world mentality. Many immigrants were flocking to America as Joseph grew from boy to man, and most brought with them a hunger to succeed in this still-young land of opportunity—opportunities denied them in their homelands. In America, if one worked hard, they could get ahead.

Both of Joseph's parents were immigrants, and both understood suffering and sacrifice.

Herman Biedenharn of Neuenkirchen, Germany, was born in 1835. Shortly afterward, his mother died. His childhood was shattered. In stepped his older brother Henry, who took on much of the child-rearing duties. (His oldest brother, Joseph, had already made a permanent move to the United States.) When Herman's father remarried in his seventies a woman Herman did not get along with, the seventeen-year-old decided he would try his own luck in America. He tried to convince his brother Henry to move with him, but to no avail. Just before he was forcefully conscripted, young Herman boarded a ship for New Orleans.

After a difficult passage, and with only $2.50 in his pocket, Herman disembarked in a new world. Within a day, the resourceful and energetic youth had a job and began working his way up the bayous and rivers of Louisiana. Sensing the rise of railroads at the expense of riverboats, Herman made his way to Monroe, Louisiana, and fell in love with the landscape and hunting. He bought a house and land and began looking for a wife to share his new home with.[181]

Four days before her tenth birthday, Louisa Wilhelmine Lundberg boarded a ship in Denmark bound for America. En route, a storm battered the ship, causing it to gradually sink. Louisa and her father watched as her mother, two younger brothers and two sisters were lowered into the angry

A Coca-Cola delivery truck at the Biedenharn Museum and Gardens in Monroe, Louisiana, by Carol Highsmith. *Library of Congress.*

sea in a lifeboat. Louisa and her father boarded the last lifeboat and joined the panic at sea.

The white-capped waves and frigid temperatures took their toll. Louisa's youngest brother, one-year-old Hans Peter, died; his distraught mother gave her youngest child to the waves.

By the time the other six Lundbergs were rescued and brought to New York City, the elements had wreaked havoc on their constitutions. Louisa's mother and her eight- and three-year-old sisters died soon after. Her last sibling, five-year-old Gustav, lasted just a little while longer before he, too, succumbed to the ordeal at sea. With all his money lost at sea, Isaak Lundberg buried his wife and four children in a potter's field.

Only he and ten-year-old Louisa remained. Father and daughter endured a seven-year odyssey with sojourns in Jackson and Vicksburg. The duo stopped in Monroe, Louisiana, on their way to a conclave of Danish immigrants in Copenhagen, Louisiana. It was a fateful stop. Louisa met her future husband, Herman Biedenharn of Neuenkirchen, Germany.[182]

Herman and Louisa were married on September 27, 1860, in Monroe, Louisiana. The Biedenharns relocated to Vicksburg, where Herman opened a shoe repair shop and then finally convinced his brother Henry to join him in America. The brothers opened a candy confectionary next door on Washington Street. Both businesses thrived, and fortunately so, for Herman and Louisa began filling their home with little ones—ten, of whom eight survived into adulthood.

When he turned eleven, Joseph went to work in his father's shoe repair shop. Though a diligent worker for his father, he was much more enthused when working for his uncle Henry at his confectionary shop. Henry was a willing tutor, and young Joseph soon mastered the arts of icing, baking and mixing sodas. So adept had Joseph become in just three years apprenticing to his uncle that he left school at fourteen to go to work full time in the confectionary shop on Washington Street.[183]

The next eight years passed amiably as Joe honed his culinary skills and uncle and nephew built their business. Then in 1888, Henry suddenly passed away. The bachelor uncle, who had happily helped his brother raise his eight children and who was often seen by passersby sitting on a rocking chair in front of the Biedenharn home, rocking a baby as he fanned it with a palmetto leaf, singing German lullabies, left his store to twenty-one-year-old Joe Biedenharn. The sign across the storefront was changed from "Biedenharn and Brother" to:

Biedenharn and Son
Wholesale and Retail Confectioners
218–220 Washington Street
Vicksburg, Mississippi[184]

Joe was now in a position to establish his own household. He began the process by courting Emma Stricker. It soon became understood that Emma was destined to become the fiancée of the young and talented confectioner.

But then the Crawford Street Methodist Church hosted a gala, and seventeen-year-old Anne Schlottman was asked to play piano for the event. When she arrived, everything was in disarray. The curtain wouldn't work, the flowers had not arrived, the lights were not working. It was chaos. The church ladies began to panic and then console each other that Joe Biedenharn could fix everything. Soon after, a six-foot-six-inch-tall twenty-two-year-old man arrived, and sure enough, the charismatic bachelor whipped everything into order, and the program thereafter ran smoothly.

It ran too smoothly for Emma Stricker, for Joe had fallen for the petite Anne Schlottman. When the program ended, he asked to escort the young lady home. The cheerful and vivacious pianist had won his heart.[185]

TRADE-MARK.

THE COCA COLA COMPANY.
NUTRIENT OR TONIC BEVERAGES.

No. 22,406.   Registered Jan. 31, 1893.

The 1893 trademark registration by the Coca-Cola Company for "Coca-Cola Brand Nutrient or Tonic Beverages." *Library of Congress.*

Torn between what he perceived as his duty to Emma but profoundly moved by his encounter with Anne, Joe wrote a letter to each young lady. Unfortunately, he placed the letters in the wrong envelopes. Learning of his unfaithfulness, Emma was furious. Understanding the mix-up, Anne laughed it off.

Embarrassed and conflicted, Joe was at a loss. Then his practical, Danish mother offered a solution: she would host a dinner party, and *both* Emma and Anne would be invited.

The unorthodox gathering was a success—at least for Joe and Anne. The couple were married the next year on July 31, 1889.

Three years later, their first child, Henry, was born. Joe then moved his young family out of his parents' house to his own on Clay Street. A year later, a second son, Malcolm was born. In 1902 and 1907, two more children would be born to Joe and Anne.

The year 1894 would forever change the Biedenharn family.

In 1886, a new carbonated drink was introduced to the public at Jacob's Pharmacy in Atlanta, Georgia: Coca-Cola. Joe already had experience mixing sugary soda drinks at his confectionary. But this new sugary concoction took the country by storm. The syrup and carbonated mixture soon found its way to soda fountains, stores and pharmacies around the nation. John Pemberton, the original creator of the Coca-Cola syrup made twenty-five gallons of the drink that first year and spent forty-six dollars in advertising. Pemberton understood the importance of marketing, but he also sensed death approaching, so he sold his syrup in 1888 to Asa Candler.

Candler was in the wholesale business, and sensing a potential bonanza in Coca-Cola, he sold his other interests and threw his $50,000 fortune behind the new drink. Within a decade, Pemberton's initial 25 gallons had grown to 214,008 gallons. Coca-Cola was here to stay.[186]

Joe Biedenharn's confectionary made a tidy profit off the hit drink. But Joe saw an even greater potential for the product. Until 1894, his customers had to make their way to downtown Vicksburg to enjoy a Coca-Cola. He proposed to take the product to them. Consequently, Joe threw his energy behind the bottling business and began to place the popular drink in bottles that he would then take to the country folk.

"I just went to work and bottled Coca-Cola there in the Washington Street store where all the soda water equipment was located. I did not say anything to Mr. Candler about it, but I did ship him the first two dozen cases of Coca-Cola I bottled."[187]

Joe was a natural salesman, a happy-go-lucky guy who endeared himself to his rural customers. He was the rare raconteur who also enjoyed listening to others. People felt comfortable in his presence. And then there was the candy he liberally dispensed on his rides through the country—and the Coca-Cola. Soon, Vicksburg and its environs were clamoring for the new drink. And they no longer had to drive to the downtown soda fountain for a glass. The glass bottles came to them.

"I delivered my bottled Coca-Cola in a dray for the trade in and near Vicksburg. The town delivery was done in cases containing four dozen bottles each. Most of the out-of-town shipping in the early days was done by boat up and down the Mississippi River and its tributaries."[188]

Soon, Coca-Cola was being marketed and sold across the globe.

An advertisement for Coca-Cola that appeared in the *Southern Churchman* magazine in 1915. *Internet Archive.*

Amalfi Coast, Italy

1926

[The Bidenharns took a family trip one summer to Italy.] *Out of this Italian loveliness a familiar sound suddenly rang in our ears. A voice called out in broken English through a megaphone, "Coca-Cola icy-cold, Icy-cold Coca-Cola. Jus'a lika in America. Stoppa here, getta Coca-Cola icy cold." Father said to the bus driver, "Take us to that voice, and I will treat everyone to a Coca-Cola." After the next hairpin bend the bus stopped. Father got out first, hugged and patted the little, fat, laughing Italian and bought ice-cold Coca-Cola for everyone....Later whenever Amalfi was mentioned, Father, with amusement in his voice, quickly added, "Coca-Cola was there, too."* [189]

Egypt

1955

As I sat high on my camel in 1955, primitive Arabs in sandals, long white robes, and flowing turbans, ran over the hot sands carrying buckets of ice and Coca-Cola. They followed me through the tombs and temples. In spirited competition they clamored for my American dollar. No nickel business here! Father would have been astounded and displeased at the price his gullible daughter paid for Coca-Cola after Coca-Cola. In the sun scorched desert Coca-Cola was a cool oasis to my parched tongue. [190]

Spain

1960s

I was often stopped by Spaniards who wanted to talk about foreign countries or their own, and if the newspapers were afraid to talk politics, the people were not. Jokes were common. Generalísimo Franco was traveling through the countryside when his coach broke down. Desiring to know what his people thought, he walked alone to a farmer and said, "How're things?" and the farmer said, "Lousy. The government doesn't know its ass from its elbow." Franco became angry and said, "Don't you know who I am?" and the farmer said, "I've seen your face somewhere before," and Franco said, "You'll find my name on all the principal streets, everywhere." The farmer dropped his hoe, looked up with delight and cried, "Oh! Señor Coca-Cola!"[191]

Joseph understood that his bottling experiment had provided generational wealth to his immigrant family. The large German Danish family became known as a bottling family as nearly everyone chipped in to promote what had become a family business. As Joseph continually told his siblings and children: "I have heard it said that Coca-Cola sells itself, that there is no real need of advertising anymore. This is not true. We've got to sell Coca-Cola and keep on selling it. There are always new markets to conquer."[192]

Joseph Biedenharn eventually moved his family to Monroe, Louisiana, where his father and mother had first met and married. The family became known for its philanthropy and civic mindedness. And its unabashed promotion of Coca-Cola.

Vintage Coca-Cola bottling equipment at the Biedenharn Coca-Cola Museum in Vicksburg. *Ryan Starrett.*

At the March 1936 Coca-Cola's Bottlers' Business Conference in Atlanta, Charles Veazey Rainwater opened with the following tribute to Joseph Biedenharn:

> *Coca-Cola, already a popular product, became more so, when it was made available to the by-ways of America through bottling. Every nook and corner could then get it. It became conveniently available to every person, wherever he might be. Instead of waiting for people to come after it, it could now be taken to the people. It was put everywhere at a popular price and then the world was told it was there.*
>
> *Joe Biedenharn was a traveling salesman for the Biedenharn Candy Company of Vicksburg. His territory was the rich Delta section of Mississippi. Joe believed in giving his customers what they wanted....It was in the early 90s. Coca-Cola was popular at Joe's soda fountain and so he decided to bottle it for his customers. Thus he became the first Coca-Cola Bottler and is still one and a darn good one!*[193]

Joseph Biedenharn passed away on October 9, 1952, at the age of eighty-five. Like so many of the immigrants who chose to make Vicksburg their home, the Biedenharns and their legacy made Vicksburg a finer city.

A Walker in Vicksburg

1931

You walk along Washington Street, the morning sun falling on your face and, below, the Yazoo River. Mist hangs over the river and Lake Centennial. Steam rises from a mill on the riverbank. A ferry cuts out into the water.

Vicksburg is your city. You came down from Kentucky like the old river men. You have lived here for two decades. You walk to know the city and the people in it. You try to recall the quote by Seneca: "We must walk outdoors.….A clear sky and fresh air strengthens the mind."

The city is waking up, and you see citizens starting their days. A truck rolls by, its bed full of country folks. They've come to the city for some excitement. Bakers walk home from three downtown bakeries, their early work finished. Three policemen stand talking. At a Black restaurant, Cannon's Jug Stompers plays from the horn of a graphophone: "Heeey—walk right in—set right down—and daddy let your mind roll on."[194]

At Speed Street, you look up at a tall, dead tree. A vine has grown up all the way to the top. Dozens of kingbirds fly around the top of the tree, their white bellies flashing in the sunlight. You listen to their sharp, shrill whistles.[195]

As you walk, you note that while many buildings along Washington Street have been well kept, others are falling down. The old buildings look stately when they're looked after. But wood just doesn't last when it's neglected.

Across the Yazoo River, on the bank of DeSoto Island, you can still make out the ruined frame of the steamboat *Wichita*. It was beached there for

A river scene in 1936, by Walker Evans. *New York Public Library.*

repairs a quarter century ago. It caught fire and was destroyed. A line of poetry comes to mind: "The worldly hopes men set their hearts upon / turn ashes, or they prosper, and anon: Like snow upon the desert's dusty face— resting a little hour or two are gone."[196]

Also on the island, an old saloon stands abandoned and overgrown with reeds. Vicksburg was known for its saloons once. Before Prohibition.

Every day, as you walk, you are confronted with sights of struggle. Everything seems to be struggling all the time. People against poverty and hunger. Buildings against humidity and decay. The seawall against the river. Boats against the current. You see triumph everywhere—but also failure.

You hear the clinking of a blacksmith at work to the west on Mulberry Street. He's working on an awning that will cover the sidewalk in front of a grocery. Though Vicksburg is modernizing, some things have to be done the old-fashioned way.

Mulberry is where you go to buy fish sometimes. You prefer catfish, like any respectable Vicksburger. But the fishmonger on Mulberry doesn't always have catfish. Sometimes, he has buffalo, the huge, fat fish with puckered mouths and wide scales. A big one could be toddler sized. Some people cut the ribs out and smoke them like pork ribs. You remember the time he tried to sell you garfish; you didn't want it. Nobody wanted it. He ended up throwing it out.[197]

You reach Glass Bayou. It's dry, and you look down into the ravine. When a bayou dries up, you can find relics embedded in the mud—a grapeshot, a Minié ball, an old, rusted-out pistol. You find these objects and wonder if, decades ago, they caused the death of some soldier.[198]

You turn toward the Yazoo River. There are a couple dozen boats moored there. Some are shantyboats and hold families, lives. You squint at one, trying to make out details. There's a little path through the willows that leads to the shantyboat. You see a man and a woman wearing drab clothes. Their cabin is tiny; you can see bunks, a couple chairs, a little table holding an oil lamp, a wood stove. These people hardly have anything— no permanence, no security. Yet they have something—a house, however modest, freedom of movement.[199]

Leaning wooden buildings along a Vicksburg street in 1936, by Walker Evans. *New York Public Library*.

In the area around the shantyboat are mud-mired boat landings, abandoned floating chicken coops, channels newly dredged—signs of the never-ending challenge of living with the river. Beyond Levee Street are willows and garbage.

You watch as the *Tennessee Belle* takes on coal at a barge. It's one of the last packet ships that travels the river. A Black man walks by. He tells you he's walking down to the dock to buy fish heads. He wants to make a stew. Buzzards list overhead. Another man, Joe, pushes an ornately decorated cart, little bells hanging off it, jingling. He's selling lollipops to ferry customers. Joe is the best whistler in Vicksburg.

Joe makes you think of Mary Dash. You haven't seen her in a while. She used to push a little four-wheeled cart around town with her name painted on the side. She sold coffee cakes and pastries door to door. You can still taste the delicious Mary Dash coffee cake you had while visiting a friend, the cake melting in your mouth as you sipped hot tea. You wonder if she's well—hope she's well.[200]

One hundred years before, a mob of Vicksburgers pulled four gamblers out of a coffeehouse near here, at a place called the Kangaroo. They

An overview of Vicksburg in 1940, by Marion Post Wolcott. *New York Public Library.*

marched them to the town square and hanged them. The act said to the rest of the nation that justice in Vicksburg was swift and mercurial. Now, there's a gas station being built.[201]

You turn back, walk south to Grove Street. At the corner of Washington and Grove is a little shack. You've always been able to buy chitterlings there—well, you were always *able* to, not that you ever wanted to. The shack is cobbled together from brick and wood, no unifying architectural vision to bring it together. The place used to sell chitterlings, but now the Black boy inside seems to be pressing clothes.[202]

You continue on to China Street, where you hear a song being sung in an exotic language.

Comme se fricceca
la luna chiena!
lo mare ride,
ll'aria è serena.

The song is coming from the mouth of Vito Canizaro, a short, fat shoemaker who works from a little shop there. He often sings. Sometimes, he plays accordion, too. He grew up in Sicily but found his way to Vicksburg.

You walk up China Street to Cherry Street. There, you see something that lifts your spirits, gets you feeling optimistic about the future. There was a row of shacks here just fifteen years ago. The shacks have been torn down, and now, modern bungalows stand. Progress—out with the old, in with the new. Vicksburg will continue to improve indefinitely, you think.[203]

You follow the streetcar tracks to Clay Street. There, beside the Hotel Vicksburg, is A.G. Lowande's novelty shop. He makes his living selling toys mostly. But this job is just temporary—many people don't realize Lowande is actually the "Adonis on the Bounding Rope." He's a professional acrobat who spent many years in Brazil. He comes from a family of acrobats going back to the American Revolution. Lowande has had close calls in his career. He has told you of the time the elephants got loose in the main tent, trampled the place, sent circusgoers running in every direction. He has told you of the injury he got last year in Kentucky and of his bad fortune joining up with a circus that folded near Vicksburg last year. That's how he ended up here.[204]

Clay Street is also where Mrs. Bonelli is cultivating a small vineyard that has attracted quite a bit of attention. Bonelli hires a Greek man, Tom Lombros, to trim her grapevines. Looking at the vines, you'd think too much

A Vicksburg street in 1936, by Walker Evans. *New York Public Library*.

was being cut away. But in the summer, they produce more fruit than ever. There's a lesson: with care, persistence and attention, grapes will grow in Vicksburg by the fat bunch.[205]

You continue on to Crawford Street, where you hear a yell: "Tost! Tost!" You know it's Bunk, the old gray-haired Black man who hobbles through the city each day selling the *Evening Post*. Bunk walks with a cane and can't speak properly. He yells, "Tost!" But he means, "Post!" You earn your living writing for the *Post*; Bunk earns his living selling it. You're both out walking, heeding Seneca's advice.[206]

Parishioners exit St. Paul's—low Mass has just let out. You see the Brothers of the Sacred Heart walking east toward St. Aloysius College. You take a moment to appreciate how the classic spire of St. Paul's rises above the other buildings around it. The sound of the church's bells fills you with an unexplainable feeling—a good feeling.

You pass by Leila Luckett's little shop. Old English letters spell out "Gift Shop Unique." You decide to step inside, see what Miss Leila is up to this day. Miss Leila's little two-story camp houses were built by her family one hundred years before, when Vicksburg was new. Trees have grown up around the houses since then—live oaks and Chinese privet. Zinnias add color to the grounds. Miss Leila points out a place in the wall where a Union cannonball once crashed through. She leads you to a room where Yankee soldiers once stabled their horses. Miss Leila's house is decorated with old paintings—portraits of family members who have passed on.[207]

You thank Miss Leila for the tour. She asks if you'll put it in your column. Vicksburgers know that if they run into you on one of your walks, they're apt to end up in print the next day.

As you walk by Fred Buckel's butcher shop, you notice a pan of cracklings sitting in the window. "These would make a nice potlikker," you think. Everyone has been talking about "potlikker" lately—that humble Southern sauce that is just the liquid leftover after boiling turnip greens or cabbages of beet greens or spinach. The *Atlanta Constitution* published an editorial arguing that cornbread should be *crumbled* into potlikker; Governor Huey P. Long of Louisiana publicly denounced the editorial, saying that cornbread should be *dunked* into potlikker. He invited the editor of the *Constitution* to New Orleans for a cornbread-dunking tournament. A war between dunkers and crumblers has begun. Potlikker—it's proof of Southern hardiness. Southerners will take something no one else likes and like it—and thrive on it.[208]

At the intersection of Speed and Drummond Streets, you take in a reminder of the racial divide in Vicksburg. Parallel to Drummond Street is a dirt road with little houses standing along it. It's a Black neighborhood, and it stands in sharp contrast to the affluent houses on Drummond Street. Morning glories climb old, faded fences, while cabbages bask in little plots. Black folks harvest the cabbages—and collards—in the fall, but the stalks are left in the field. They bunch them up, and in the spring, they produce little shoots and leaves. The new growth is good to eat until the new cabbages and collards come in. A Black woman stands on the porch of one of the houses, smoking a pipe and looking at you.[209]

You take for granted that Vicksburg's Black residents live a materially poorer life than the white people in Vicksburg. Well, most of the white people; there are those hobos, the shantyboat flotsam, the bumpkins who ride in from the county. You notice every day that Black people are poorer, and you frequently write about their condition in your column. You describe the people you see in minute detail: "There on a back gallery a tiny negro girl in a red headpiece scrubs heroicly on a washboard….One old and emaciated black woman is talking to someone inside. Spying us she halts, and after a pause a grotesque male head looks out to see who it is." But you write about

Vicksburg men sitting on a bench outside a barbershop, by Walker Evans. *New York Public Library.*

them with a mocking tone. You re-create their dialect phonetically: "Ah seed huh jes' d' utah day, en she look so well!"[210]

A thought creeps into your mind: Vicksburg is only seventy years removed from slavery. You still see—even talk to—people who were born into slavery. "We cannot help but muse what might have been for some of these men had things been different for them in the beginning," you think. You push the thought from your mind.[211]

Back at Washington Street, you notice a string of rabbits hanging in front of D.A. Bove's store. These rabbits are dead; the little white ones in the window of the feed store are alive. They share their space with little chicks. You think again about Seneca. Life seems to pass by too quickly.[212]

You see few strangers on the street here. You walk every day and talk to whomever you can. You notice Charles Feldman walking briskly (he always does), and J.M. Fried walking behind him, fingers on his ever-present cigar. You see Charles Rafferty scowling, Clum Hamilton chatting to another man on the corner.[213]

At Washington and Bridge Streets, you are pulled in by two smells: fresh-baked bread and hot tamales. The bread smell is coming from Koestler's Bakery, the Vicksburg institution that created Mello-Toast, sliced it and packaged it and sent it out to the citizens of the city and beyond. Across the street from Koester's is a humbler operation: a pushcart selling hot tamales manned by two Mexican boys who look like twins. A little farther north, Seay's Grill adds the smell of waffles to the air. Seay's calls itself "The Homelike Restaurant" and asks customers, "Tell us the way you like it." "We guarantee to please," they assure. You can get lunch for a quarter at Seay's.[214]

As you look around, you appreciate how Vicksburg is a city of trees. All around you stand crepe myrtles, pears, japonicas, wisterias, plums, persimmons, lindens, black walnuts, live oaks—not to mention the many colorful forsythias, japonicas, jonquils, irises and other flowers the city's homeowners plant. Bulbs are always available, sitting in storefront windows on Washington Street. Calvin Barber is one of those who makes an effort to cultivate interesting plants. Outside his little cottage grow clematis, sweet bays, jasmines, zinnias, hydrangeas, coxcombs, acacias and some Japanese shrubs you don't even know the names of.[215]

You decide to walk east, down Henry Street, to the railroad yards. The Yazoo and Mississippi Valley Railroad employs more than nine hundred people in Vicksburg, paying out nearly $2 million in salaries annually. Unscrupulous Vicksburgers had figured out that a company with such deep pockets could pay out a lot, not just in salaries, but also in personal injury claims. Vicksburg had become a problem for the Y&MV Railroad; it was being sued by Vicksburgers more frequently than it was by citizens of Memphis and New Orleans combined.[216]

Hobos have been camping at the railroad yards, and you notice one approaching as you walk toward the yards. He wears a small mustache

Inside a Vicksburg seed store, by Walker Evans. *New York Public Library.*

and beard, standing out blonde on his fat face. As you come face to face with him, he asks, "Do you know where I could find some work?" You've heard that at the railyards, the hobos pool the food they've managed to scrounge and cook "mulligan stew." They sit and talk about communism. Or if they've been lucky enough to eat plenty, they just sit quietly. Hunger is a wolf that stalks these men; this one had a fat face, but you've often noticed gaunt, unshaven men hanging around outside the bakery, hoping for alms of biscuits.[217]

The city doesn't want hobos and fines them five dollars for sleeping in the wrong place or being drunk on the street. The judge will tell them, "If you want to live in Vicksburg, you have to work." But it seems, based on the number of hobos you encounter each day, there isn't enough work to go around. You've heard that in some places, hobos are pressed into cotton-picking gangs.

At the railyards, you find your mood turning dark. So, you leave that place. You hear a droning sound far overhead. You think some men are hungry, and some men are traveling in the sky. Every day at noon, you see this red-tailed monoplane fly over the city from the east and cross the river. You hear its engine and want to know: Who is in there? You know everyone in Vicksburg, talk to everyone. But the pilot is too high up. Airplanes, motorboats zipping along the Yazoo—you still remember when everyone got around on horses. You can still spot the places on China Street where a dozen liveries used to operate. Now, there is just Ray Lum's place. Lum loves horses, keeps Norman horses and breeds Hereford cattle. Lum withstood the shift to automobiles and is now the place in town where lovers of horses can congregate.[218]

You think, "So much has changed in my lifetime. What will Vicksburg look like in another twenty years? Another fifty? Another hundred?"

You feel unsettled. In any case, this walk has given you plenty to write about. You head back toward Crawford Street, to the *Vicksburg Evening Post* building. From the windows of the building, you might look down on the river for a few more minutes, ruminate on what you've experienced before sitting down to write.

THE BAD MAN

Rafael McCloud and Vicksburg's Week of Fear

MARCH 2, 2016

Elizabeth Keen stepped out of her mom's car, into the cool morning air. Keen was an eighth grader at St. Aloysius, and she followed the same routine each day: wake up early, ride from Redwood twenty minutes into town with her mom, a teacher at the school. She would then make her way through the elementary school on her way to the middle school. But this morning, something seemed off.

"We were just going inside to start the day, and one of the teachers was at the door letting people in, kind of being weird. Like he'd kind of guard it almost," Keen said.

The teacher was Peter Pikul, a high school theology teacher and longtime leader at St. Aloysius. Pikul was standing, watching, at the entrance to the elementary school. That wasn't normal.

Keen walked downstairs, through the elementary school, toward the middle school. She passed the elementary school classrooms, the science labs, the big windows of the library. She passed into a small outdoor area with a picnic table. Again, a teacher stood guard at the door. This time, it was biology teacher Dawn Meeks.

"She's standing by the door....She goes to unlock it," Keen said. "I'm like, these doors are open every day. We walk in and out like there's no problem."

Keen remembers stopping and questioning Meeks.

"What's going on?"

"Well, you didn't hear? This guy escaped from prison this morning."

It was the first Keen had heard of what would become an infamous week in Vicksburg history. Accused murderer Rafael McCloud had broken out of jail early that morning. He had held a guard at knifepoint, taken his radio, his clothes, his keys, and disappeared into a city that he knew well.

And the staff of St. Aloysius had reason to be afraid—Warren County Jail, from which McCloud had escaped, was less than a mile down Grove Street. The following seven days would go down as some of the tensest and most unsettling in Vicksburg's modern history. Vicksburg's citizens would spend the week peering nervously out of windows, locking doors—and then double checking them—and scouring the papers for information about McCloud.

Has he been caught? Where could he be? What could he do?[219]

Rafael McCloud was the last person anyone would want to be loose in Vicksburg. He had been charged the year before with the gruesome murder of Sharen Wilson, a beloved sixty-nine-year-old grandmother. The macabre details of the murder had shocked and wounded the community. *How could such an evil fate befall someone so good?*

Wilson was from Hammond, Louisiana. But she and her husband had made friends in Vicksburg. They liked the city enough to relocate there after Hurricane Katrina in 2005. Wilson was captivated by a stately nineteenth-century house on Drummond Street. She moved into the house with her husband, Dixon, and got her dream car, too, a black Mercedes convertible. Wilson spent her time gardening—a friend told a reporter that Wilson could root a plant faster than anyone—and working in Peterson's Art and Antiques downtown. Wilson had a keen eye for decorating and put thought and care into arranging—and rearranging—the shop. She attended St. Michael Catholic Church and did water aerobics at the YMCA.[220]

Wilson's husband passed away in 2012, leaving her alone in a city she had come to love. But it just didn't feel like home without her partner. She decided to move back to Hammond. She listed her house. But no one seemed eager to buy it. Wilson waited for the house to sell. She waited and waited, for two years.

Wilson was a kind person who nurtured and improved others and made friends and connections. Rafael McCloud was the opposite. He stole from an early age. He was arrested at twenty for auto burglary, at twenty-one for embezzlement, at twenty-four for armed robbery.

The armed robbery charge came in 2005. McCloud used a knife to rob a man of his wallet, watch, change, credit cards and fifteen dollars in cash. A warrant went out for his arrest, but he hid out for a month and then fled down West Magnolia Street when an officer tried to arrest him. Police found him hiding underneath a house. The incident showed who McCloud was: a violent, wily criminal with a penchant for knives who would go to dramatic lengths to avoid capture. His previous convictions for auto burglary and grand larceny (reduced from two counts of felony embezzlement) and the new charge of armed robbery resulted in jail time for McCloud. He was sentenced to ten years in prison.

But he would get credit for time served and had to spend only four of the ten years behind bars, Judge Isadore Patrick ordered. The remaining five years would be spent under supervised release. McCloud was sentenced in May 2006. Had he still been in prison nine years later, Wilson would have passed another routine day. She would have been one day closer to moving back to Hammond, one day closer to reuniting with her family. But that was not the case.[221]

Instead, McCloud was out, a free man who furtively observed Wilson retrieve a spare key from a hidden spot outside her home the night of Saturday, June 27, 2015. McCloud waited for Wilson to put the key back in its hiding place. She entered her home. Then he retrieved the key and entered her house. McCloud carried a .40-caliber pistol that he had stolen the month before in a burglary. He attacked her in her kitchen. A *Vicksburg Post* article later summarized what happened next in terse, heartbreaking terms: "Police say Wilson was stalked, tied up, raped, abducted and taken to an abandoned hospital where she was shot in the head with a stolen gun."[222]

Wilson's life had ended in a horrific place, the abandoned Kuhn Memorial Hospital. The hospital, originally built in 1832, had treated yellow fever patients, Civil War wounded, the criminally insane and countless others before being shuttered in 1989. Since then, it had sat abandoned, falling apart, eventually attracting scholars of the macabre, who described it reliably as something straight out of a horror movie. In 2014, *Clarion-Ledger* reporter Therese Apel filmed a ghost-hunting excursion through the hospital. The same year, the reality TV show *Ghost Asylum* filmed an episode there. It had become one of the United States most notorious abandoned buildings.

By the time the sun was beginning to rise on Sunday, June 28, McCloud had left Wilson's body at the hospital, picked up his nephew Akeem and driven Wilson's Nissan Murano halfway up the Delta to Leland. Leland police stopped McCloud for reckless driving at 8:30 a.m. and realized he was driving Wilson's stolen car. They also found the stolen .40-caliber pistol. Not knowing yet that Wilson had been murdered, they contacted Vicksburg police and asked if they could check on her. Vicksburg PD knocked on her door—no answer. Later that morning, a neighbor, alarmed after Wilson's family in Hammond said they weren't able to reach her, entered Wilson's house and realized it had been ransacked. Police returned and confirmed that something terrible had happened to Wilson.

In Leland, McCloud told police that he had dropped her off in Greenville earlier that morning. He directed police on a journey to the city. On the way, they got a call: Wilson's body had been found—by ghost hunters of all people. A trail of blood leading into the hospital told them that Wilson had been alive as McCloud dragged her inside.[223]

Within a few hours of the killing of Wilson, police had investigated the crime scene, caught the murderer and found the body and the murder weapon. By Monday morning, the citizens of Vicksburg were learning the details of the horrific crime.

Elizabeth Keen sat in the cafeteria with other middle schoolers at St. Aloysius. For thirty minutes, students gathered in the cafeteria to say prayers and hear announcements. They prayed the Our Father, the Hail Mary and the aspiration, "St. Aloysius, pray for us." And they shared bits of information about the escaped murder suspect who was somewhere in town. He'd made his own weapon from a piece of his bed. He'd taken a guard's clothes. They'd found his shoes on the street near the school.

"At least that was the rumor," Keen said.

The doors into St. Aloysius remained locked. Keen remembers going to theology class that morning, "freaked out." She was told no one could leave class for the bathroom or any other reason. Her worried feeling was ratcheted up when she looked out her classroom's window, toward a courtyard, and saw Vicksburg police walking across the school grounds with German shepherds. Another girl in class screamed.

"I remember our teacher saying, 'It's OK—isn't it better that they're here? They're helping us,'" Keen said.

A boardwalk across Grant's Canal, by Carol Highsmith. *Library of Congress.*

The sight of the police started a new rumor through the school: dogs had followed McCloud's trail across the football field. Rumors shifted. He'd gotten to the military park. He was at Fred's department store. He'd vowed to kill as many people as he could before being recaptured.

Keen passed that first day in lockdown, a cloud of nervous dread hanging over everyone. After school, she rode home with her mom. They talked about McCloud and scanned the scenery passing by the car windows. *Is he there, in the woods? Or there?*

The next day, the front page of the *Vicksburg Post* was covered with stories about McCloud's escape, with one enormous headline telling citizens the most important fact: "Still Loose."

Vicksburg-Warren County public schools were locked down as well. School staff around the city inspected their buildings carefully before the start of the day. Any neglected closet, any seldom-used space, any outbuilding could be a potential hiding spot. When given the all-clear, staff watched streets and parking lots throughout the day.[224]

Keen's school had been filled with rumors, and it was a microcosm of the city itself. Since McCloud had escaped, police had been fielding rumors of sightings. One person claimed they saw him in the military park. Others had seen him in their neighborhoods. Each time they got a tip, officers went to check it out. Vicksburg police had been joined by officers from the Warren County Sheriff's Department; Mississippi Bureau of Investigation; Mississippi Bureau of Narcotics; Wildlife, Fisheries and Parks; and the U.S. Marshals Service. The Mississippi Highway Patrol flew over Vicksburg in a helicopter, pointing infrared down into stands of trees.

They headed for Sky Farm Avenue, where some of McCloud's family lived. At one point, police thought they had him pinned down at the Dixiana Hotel on South Washington Street. They converged on the hotel wearing tactical gear. Turns out, he wasn't there. The large police presence evinced a fact about the situation: McCloud was a particularly deranged kind of criminal and was still presumably armed with the shank he'd used to escape. Each minute that McCloud remained at large added to the probability that more innocent Vicksburgers could become victims. Officer Joseph Stubbs traveled around Vicksburg, handing out mugshots and impressing this fact onto business owners and citizens.

"He's already hurt one person, and she was a lady and an employee of a downtown store," he told a reporter. "She was a very good friend and I miss her."[225]

The next day, March 4, the *Post* published a single, page-filling image on its front page. It was McCloud's mugshot. Overlaid text told readers that he had still not been caught: "The Search for Rafael."

Police continued to focus on Northeast Vicksburg but expanded their search into Warren County and Louisiana. They combed through Kuhn Memorial Hospital, where he had left Sharen Wilson's body five years before. At Kuhn, they found a vital clue: the green pants McCloud had taken off the Warren County Jail guard on the morning of his escape. McCloud was most likely still in the city, creeping around the grimy hideouts he knew best.[226]

Another day passed. Police felt McCloud was most likely still in Vicksburg. He hadn't had any money or means of leaving town when he escaped. Unless someone had helped him, he was probably still around. Police stressed to the community: if you help him, you will be punished to the full extent of the law.

Students in Vicksburg began to relax. *He couldn't still be here, right? He had to be far away by now. He's in Mexico. Right?*

The Dixiana Motel, where police thought they had cornered Rafael McCloud. *Library of Congress.*

By Sunday, March 6, despite searching for four days and nights, police still had not located McCloud. Local businesses—Fox's Pizza, the Salvation Army, the Red Cross, Ameristar Casino, McDonald's—coordinated a supply effort to keep the massive search effort well fed. Warren County Sheriff Martin Pace spoke to *Vicksburg Post* reporter John Surratt: "We have looked everywhere and we're still doing double shifts. It's possible he may have left town, but we're going to keep looking here until we can get information verified that he is no longer here."[227]

Three more days passed with no leads. Police had expanded their search to Claiborne County, Mississippi, and Madison Parish, Louisiana. It had been a week since McCloud escaped. Then it was all over.

Around 4:00 a.m. on Thursday, March 10, Rafael McCloud did something he had done before: entered the home of innocent, unsuspecting people with the intent to do them harm. McCloud turned the doorknob of a home on Fort Hill Drive. It was unlocked. He crept inside and found a couple already awake, getting ready for their workday. They had a five-year-old.

The father fought McCloud. The mother fought McCloud. He stabbed the father and smashed the mother's head. McCloud was able to overpower the couple and bind them, as he had bound Sharen Wilson five years earlier.

He forced them into their bathroom. Mercifully, the child was allowed to stay with his parents.

It seemed like Vicksburg would suffer another horrific wound. But this time, the story took a different turn. The mother was able, somehow, to escape her restraints. She escaped the bathroom, found her gun and then found McCloud. She shot him and untied her husband. He also shot McCloud several times, putting a bullet into his brain for good measure.[228]

The family ran out to the street and flagged down a passing driver. Police arrived at 7:00 a.m. In the bathtub of the home lay the body of the man who had unsettled Vicksburg for a year. He was wearing "nice, white tennis shoes," police told reporters. "A pair of blue jeans." They thought someone had aided him in the previous days.

It was the day of National Junior Honor Society inductions at St. Aloysius. Elizabeth Keen was dressed in her "Mass uniform," a white blouse and patterned skirt, more formal than her normal khakis and polo. Parents would be there to watch their kids be inducted into the society. She and her fellow inductees would walk out on stage with candles. The ceremony would be held in the gym.

"We were put in the foyer room, by the front door," Keen said. "We were all lined up down the hallway in the order we had to walk in."

Parents, family, friends were entering the gym all at once.

"That's when someone started yelling, 'Rafael's dead! Rafael's dead! Somebody killed him!'"

Information moved through the gym. He had taken homeowners hostage. The homeowners had shot him. Keen felt relief. "Thank God he's not going to come kill us," she said. But the feeling of relief was tinged with one final sickening realization: he had been in the city the whole time.

The ordeal would be remembered by the *Post* as the biggest story of the year, a threat to the community that had, nonetheless, galvanized it. Rafael McCloud would be remembered ever after with scorn. And the day that he died would be remembered as the day a miserable man was put out of his misery.

THE OAK

"Across the River and Under the Shade of the Tree"

The acorn took root in soil high on a bluff. Over the next two hundred years, it would grow taller and stronger. It would be shaken and damaged and nearly destroyed. It would drop its own acorns to the ground.

For the next two hundred years, the oak would grow alongside a shaken and damaged and nearly destroyed city.

For more than two centuries, the oak and Vicksburg would evolve and endure side by side.[229]

In 1797, Andrew Glass, a noted Natchez Trace bandit, built a two-story house in Spanish territory at Nogales, or Walnut Hills. Though American, Glass recognized the benefits of a domicile inside the disputed borderlands. He also recognized the risks. So, he built his two-story home (a bedroom atop a kitchen) without a staircase to access the bedroom. Instead, Glass would raise and lower himself by rope or ladder and thus create a convenient way to avoid ambush.

Just a year later, the United States asserted its authority over Natchez and Fort Nogales. Andrew Glass was now residing on U.S. soil. No longer living on a convenient border for a land pirate, Glass met the inevitable fate of a highwayman when he was shot during a robbery. He was pursued to his home in Walnut Hills, where he managed to elude his captors but succumbed to his wounds later that night, beneath the shadow of the oak tree.[230]

Mary Elizabeth Howard

August 30, 1836

The oak had endured another Mississippi winter, spring and summer. New residents occupied Andrew Glass's house. A newer one was due later that day.

Mary Elizabeth Howard lay in a state of pain and panic. She had been married for three years and was delivering her first child at fifteen. Her husband, Sheriff Stephen Howard, had just bought and added to Glass's hideaway. The Howard house boasted a new dining room and a middle bedroom where Mary was now determined to birth her first child. Her prized quilt, painstakingly and lovingly stitched by her grandmother and given to her as a wedding gift, lay folded away from the birthing area. Her ivory-handled opera glasses, white gloves, makeup kit, silver brush and ceramic bowl lay on her dresser, all awaiting her attention once the trauma of birth subsided and she again enjoyed Vicksburg's social scene with her husband.

After a long and complicated delivery, a baby's wail could be heard under the shade of the tree. Stephen and Mary Elizabeth Howard were the proud parents of a daughter they named Caren.

Days later, the local paper carried the following notice: "Friends and acquaintances of the late Mary E. Howard attend her funeral to-morrow at three o'clock, P.M.…at the old family burying ground…the procession to take place from S. Howard's plantation, three miles below Vicksburg."[231]

A distraught Sheriff Howard resigned his post and moved to Yazoo City. Five years later, he joined his wife in death.[232]

Confederate Hospital

May 18, 1863–July 4, 1863

The ground outside the McRaven House was filled with bodies.[233] Some dead, and others on their way to being dead—but more were wishing they were already dead as the limbs began to pile up.

The Andrew Glass room at the McRaven House. *Ryan Starrett*.

The field outside McRaven House where the Confederate makeshift hospital would have been. *Ryan Starrett*.

McRaven House in 2023. *Ryan Starrett.*

"Three men have just had their limbs amputated. This is so common that it is scarcely noticed."[234]

The house had already been struck by several cannonballs, as the siege had been going on for weeks. It would go on for a total of forty-seven days. With each passing day, more wounded would be brought to makeshift hospitals like that at the McRaven House. Its owner, John Bobb, watched as his yard, which had been filled with roses, now filled with the dead and amputees. The smell of roses had been replaced by the smell of human rot and decay.

"A stream of blood ran from the table into a tub in which was the arm. It had been taken off at the socket, and the hand was hanging over the edge of the tub, a lifeless thing."[235]

The continuous sound of cannon fire was accompanied by the groans and screams coming from the front yard, the sound of saws grating through bones, the surgeons shouting, "Hold him down! Hold him down!" There was also the *thunk* of arms and legs being tossed into tubs, the prayers and supplications of ministers and those begging for the pain to stop, a constant cacophony of suffering.

And that was just the aural symphony the Bobbs were subjected to. Should any wander outside, the horror of the sight matched the intensity of the sounds.

"There is a [man] from Georgia shot through the head. A curtain is drawn across a corner where he is lying to hide the hideous spectacle, as his brains are oozing out."[236]

Visual and tangible senses now verified the disembodied sounds of suffering that had haunted the house and grounds. The hellish scene would continue until the end of the siege and fall of Vicksburg.

Less than a year after Vicksburg fell, another body would lay dying on the grounds, this time with no surgeon to dress his wounds, only a wife to weep over his corpse.

⁌

THE MURDER OF JOHN BOBB

May 18, 1864

In the shadow of the tree, John Bobb stood on his eleven acres chatting with his friend, Mr. Mattingly. Bobb was proud of his estate, especially the house he had bought from his brother twenty years before. He had added an Italianate section to the front and had filled the yard with the rose bushes his wife, Celina, so adored.[237] The Bobbs had weathered the siege of Vicksburg and were adjusting to life under Federal control.

Perhaps the biggest adjustment was the sight of hundreds of armed former enslaved people wearing the Union blue. Such a troop now entered Bobb's yard and began cutting roses. Bobb cursed them and ordered them to leave immediately. The soldiers cursed back and threatened to do more than damage bushes. Bobb picked up a brick and hurled it at the company, striking one. The soldiers left, promising to return.

Bobb and Mattingly left the yard with the oak tree, magnolias and roses to report the matter to the occupying commander, General Henry Slocum, and to ask for a guard to protect his property.

While her husband awaited a word with the commander, Celina noticed a group of soldiers had returned and were awaiting the return of her husband. She promptly sent a young girl to apprise him of the situation. But Bobb and his companion had returned—without a guard—by a different path and ran directly into twenty-five Union soldiers. The unit marched Bobb one hundred yards away to Stouts Bayou.

Celina heard nine gunshots in succession and ran to the creek. Seven shots had been fired at Mattingly as he fled to safety. But the first two bullets had found their mark—one in John Bobb's head, the other in his heart.

Celina wept over her husband's body and then had it brought back past the rose bushes, under the shade of the oak and into their house to prepare it for his funeral.[238]

∽

The Great Flood

May 3, 1927

The Mound Landing crevasse, one hundred miles north of Vicksburg, had ruptured on April 21, 1927, and immediately began flooding the Yazoo River Basin. Much of Greenville was already underwater, and the flood continued its inexorable move south, reentering the Mississippi River at Vicksburg. Madison Parish, across the river from Vicksburg, decided to breach its own levee at Cabin Teele with the intent of allowing the water pressure to weaken and preserve as much of the levee as possible. The levee would then be repaired when the waters subsided. The wooded topography would help to slow the floodwaters. The *Vicksburg Evening Post* thereafter reported: "Trees alongside the break, and the 'buck shot' dirt are serving to retard the crumpling of the levees, thus holding narrow the outlet for the angry waters in that section."[239]

Carneal "Blue" Woodyear, a Madison Parish resident and onetime sheriff, recalled, "I was close by when it broke. Everyone knew it was coming and was pretty well packed up and ready to head to high ground. A lot of people went to Vicksburg. You could hear the steamboats coming down the river at night with boatloads of people on them. There was boatload after boatload of refugees going to Vicksburg."[240]

The Flood of 1927 finally crested in Vicksburg at 56.2 feet. (The river would not reach that height again until the Flood of 2011, when it crested at 57.1 feet.)

Vicksburg's position on the bluffs was its salvation, as the bulk of the city was saved. Those same bluffs, however, resulted in Vicksburg being chosen as headquarters for the Red Cross relief services and the destination of thousands of refugees who would soon call Vicksburg's levee "home."

While the poorer refugees waited and waited for the waters to recede on the levee in the increasingly hot Mississippi sun, the oak tree at the McRaven house had survived another natural disaster.

Its ultimate survival test would come twenty-six years later.

But first, the tree, the house and the grounds of McRaven would have to endure an eccentric and negligent pair of sisters.

THE MURRAY FAMILY

1882–1960

Northerners now occupied the house. William Murray, a soldier in General Ulysses Grant's army, moved to Vicksburg after the war. In 1882, he bought the McRaven House and moved his five children into their new home. Within four years, he would add two more to his brood.

Murray made his living as a carriage-maker and quickly ingratiated himself into Vicksburg society. By the time of his death in 1911, he was a member of the Knights of Pythias, Masons, Woodmen and the Independent Order of Odd Fellows. After months of battling a severe illness, William Murray died and was buried in Cedar Hill Cemetery.[241]

His wife of forty-six years, Ellen, would remain at the McRaven House with her two unmarried daughters, Ella and Annie. Ten years later, she joined her husband at Cedar Hill.[242]

Now, Ellie and Annie, aged forty-two and thirty-eight, respectively, and still unmarried, continued their spinster existence at the McRaven House.[243] The two grew increasingly isolated and eccentric. They cut off nearly all contact aside from their doctor. They even began to live in the living room only, where they moved their shared bed. Former McRaven caretaker Leonard Fuller explained: "They moved their bed in here. They were old and they didn't want to go up and down the steps. The last two years of their lives, the sisters couldn't stand the cold so they cooked in the fireplace. To get to the old kitchen, you have to go outside. They chopped up antique furniture for firewood."[244]

In a scene eerily similar to the famed Goat Castle of Natchez, the two aging sisters allowed the house and grounds to fall apart around them as they lived an increasingly meager and frugal existence. Leonard added: "As the ladies got older, a good bit of their diet was sardines. They saved every single sardine can they ever used; there were sardine cans everywhere."[245]

In 1960, Ellen died at eighty-one. Her sister then sold the family home and moved into a nursing home.

The McRaven House disappeared deeper into the landscape, and vines entirely covered the upper story.

The house was sold to O.E. Bradway in 1960, and then to Charles and Sandra Harvey in 1979, before it was bought by mustard magnate Leyland French in 1984. In 2015, the house was bought by Kendra and Steven Reed. With each owner, the McRaven House would go through another set of renovations, always maintaining its "time capsule" feel.

The oak tree would remain the same. Just another year older.

The Vicksburg Tornado

December 5, 1953

What sounded like "an express train on Mulberry Street" roared through the air. "It suddenly became black, then big drops of rain fell for just a second."[246] The waters of the Mississippi River began to whitecap. The air turned into a pressure cooker. Trees began to sway. *The* tree began to shake and sway to its foundation. The limbs of lesser trees began to snap. And then their trunks. Still, the tornado, which had formed over the Yazoo River, gathered strength.

Soon enough, the tempest was in the heart of the city, destroying older buildings, playing with newer, damaging all. The tornado raged through Vicksburg's business district as shoppers, businessmen and passersby ran for cover.

Moments later, the F-5 tornado, the fifth deadliest in Mississippi history, moved on, leaving Vicksburg again looking like a war zone. Twelve blocks lay in ruins. St. Paul Catholic Church, built in 1849; the Illinois Central Roadhouse; the Levee Street Foundry, from South Street to Crawford Street; the Mulberry Street block; and Vicksburg Transfer Company's big warehouse were all damaged, 937 buildings in all. More than one thousand people drifted about, now homeless.[247] And then the temperature dropped to thirty-one degrees—with the utilities nonfunctional.

Beneath the rubble lay 38 dead. Another 270 were injured to varying degrees.[248]

That afternoon, the resilient citizens of Vicksburg began the long process of rebuilding a town that had suffered worse damage in the past.

The equally resilient oak still stood as countless limbs, trees and building materials were taken to the burgeoning trash heaps in and around town.

Apotheosis

May 4, 2024

A young man sat in the shade, beneath the oak outside the McRaven House.[249] He dined on a dozen Solly's tamales and a Coca-Cola, and he reflected.

This oak tree is the perfect representation of Vicksburg. This landscape the perfect motif.

Fort St. Pierre, Nogales, Walnut Hills, the homestead of Newton Vick, the Gibraltar of the Confederacy, the Red Carpet City of the South, the Key to the South.

The rich and suave man fell into a bluff-sized doldrum reflecting on Vicksburg's history: the usurpation of the land, retaliatory vengeance, the murder of a local doctor and consequent lynching of a number of known gamblers, slavery, the Civil War, the Redeemers, the lynching of Lloyd Clay, Prohibition. An entire catalogue of Vicksburg's manifold crimes paraded through his mind.

The sun was up, and a humid Mississippi summer seeped into his shirt. Sweat ran down his back. A slight, cooling breeze rippled through the foliage above and around him.

Tamales from Solly's Tamales. *Ryan Starrett.*

Another barrage of images second-lined through his mind, images from when he began researching *The Hidden History of Vicksburg*: the River, the beauty, the diversity, The Biscuit Company, The Tomato Place, 10 South, the Lower Mississippi River Museum, Vicksburg National Military Park, the riverfront murals, the drives up and down Highway 69 and back across the Mississippi River bridge on I-20, the books and articles consulted, the houses and museums toured, the people interviewed.

The reflective and hungry man looked around as the spices from Solly's tamales reached his tastebuds, and the subsequent sip of a Coca-Cola from Biedenharn's museum added its own bite.

He looked to his left and saw the house. The house had at once been historic and progressive. It was initially built for the most practical of reasons: utility and protection. The house has since become a tourist destination for historians and ghost hunters. The house continues to defy time by becoming a microcosm of the Deep South: past and future.

He looked to his right and saw the pathway leading into the house. The greenness. The thick greenness. The greenness of Vicksburg. Green everywhere. Green, the color of purgatory, the color of hope. The color of Vicksburg.

He looked behind and saw a long line of scoundrels, heroes, villains and saints. Choctaw, French, Spanish, Chinese, Syrian and Hispanic, white and Black. All dead—some regrettably, others fortunately. Some were contributors, others destroyers. But all were part of the history, the essence, the very fabric of Vicksburg, formed, damned and saved in a unique city on a bluff that once controlled the mightiest of rivers.

He looked ahead and saw a new, even longer line of scoundrels and heroes, villains and saints. More Choctaw, French, Spanish, Chinese, Syrian and Hispanic, white and Black. And there were new people, not yet discernible—people who would come and make Vicksburg home, drawn to the opportunity and beauty of the river town. And when the river shifts again, as it inevitably will, the residents, the people, will remain. The good and bad, the movers and the moved, the great, the forgotten the forgotten great—all a part of the human drama, for better or for worse, a part of Vicksburg.

He looked down and saw the fertile ground. The land that entombed human and plant remains, amputated arms and desiccated roses and the roots of the enduring oak.

He looked above and saw the green leaves swaying in a near cloudless sky. The leaves that lived and died in a single season on the branches of a tree that had lived over two hundred years.

He unwrapped another tamale and took another sip of Coca-Cola and wished that, like the tree, he could observe and live two centuries of Vicksburg's history, with its concomitant comedy, tragedy, horror and triumph. But mostly, he wanted to witness the long pageant of human stories that went into making a city like Vicksburg so intoxicating.

NOTES

Chapter 1

1. This vignette comes from three sources: Jesuit Online Library, "Woodstock Letters, Volume LVIII, Number 1, 1 February 1929," https:// jesuitonlinelibrary.bc.edu/?a=d&d=wlet19290201-01.2.3&e=-------en-20--1-- txt-txIN------; Penicaut, *Fleur de Lys and Calumet*, 98–99; *Encyclopedia of Arkansas*, "Nicholas Foucault," https://encyclopediaofarkansas.net/entries/nicolas-foucault-7912/.
2. Technically, the French settled in "Old Biloxi" in modern-day Ocean Springs. They would later move the capital to present-day Biloxi in 1720.
3. Penicaut, *Fleur de Lys and Calumet*, 216.
4. At different times, it is also referred to as Fort St. Claude and Yazoo Post.
5. Vicksburg's Old Court House Museum, https://oldcourthouse.org/warren-county-statehood/st-pierre-fort/. The environs of Fort St. Pierre in 1720 were similar to that of New Orleans.
6. Vicksburg's Old Court House Museum, https://oldcourthouse.org/warren-county-statehood/st-pierre-fort/.
7. French, *Historical Collections Louisiana*, 43–46. French's account in this chapter is a translation of the memoirs of Dumont de Montigny.
8. French, *Historical Collections Louisiana*, 72.
9. French, *Historical Collections Louisiana*, 77.
10. French, *Historical Collections Louisiana*, 78–79.
11. Myers, *1729*, 174.
12. French, *Historical Collections Louisiana*, 74.

13. Make peace.

14. Jesuit Online Library, "Woodstock Letters."

15. Briuer, "300ᵗʰ Anniversary."

16. Briuer, "300ᵗʰ Anniversary."

17. French, *Historical Collections of Louisiana*, 3:154–55.

18. Myers, *1729*, 195.

19. Myers, *1729*, 197–200.

Chapter 2

20. Robert F. Moss, *Barbecue: The History of an American Institution* (Tuscaloosa: University of Alabama Press, 2010), 48–50; Zach Myers, "Barbecue as a Historical Looking Glass," *Legacy* 18, no. 1 (2018): n.p.

21. "Regular Toasts," *Vicksburg Whig*, July 16, 1835; "Fourth of July Dinner," *Vicksburg Whig*, June 25, 1835; "Vicksburg Prices Current," *Vicksburg Whig*, June 25, 1835.

22. "Domestic," *The Weekly Mississippian*, July 17, 1835; "The Gambler's Fate," *Vicksburg Whig*, August 13, 1835 (reprinted from the *Hamilton* [OH] *Intelligencer*).

23. "Domestic," *The Weekly Mississippian*.

24. Joshua D. Rothman, "The Hazards of the Flush Times: Gambling, Mob Violence, and the Anxieties of America's Market Revolution," *Journal of American History* 95, no. 3 (2008): 651–77.

25. Pamela Lea Grillis, *Vicksburg and Warren County: A History of People and Place* (Vicksburg, MI: Dancing Rabbit Books, 1992), 38–39.

26. Rothman, "Hazards of the Flush Times," 651–77.

27. Grillis, *Vicksburg and Warren County*, 40–43.

28. Rothman, "Hazards of the Flush Times," 651–77.

29. Rothman, "Hazards of the Flush Times," 651–77; "America—New York…," *Aris's Birmingham Gazette, Etc.*, August 31, 1835.

30. "Domestic," *The Weekly Mississippian*.

31. Rothman, "Hazards of the Flush Times," 651–77.

32. "At a Meeting of the Citizens of Warren County…," *The Weekly Natchez Courier*, July 8, 1935.

33. "Vicksburg Outrage," *Niles' Weekly Register*, August 1, 1835.

34. "The Vicksburg Gamblers," *The North Star*, November 30, 1835.

35. Rothman, "Hazards of the Flush Times," 651–77; "America—New York…," *Aris's Birmingham Gazette, Etc.*

36. Abraham Lincoln, *Famous Speeches of Abraham Lincoln* (New York: Peter Pauper Press, 1935), 4–5.

Chapter 3

37. "Fatal Encounter with a Whale," *Vicksburg Whig*, April 22, 1844. A search for the name "Edwin" in Newspaper.com's archives of the *Vicksburg Daily Whig* and *Tri-Weekly Sentinel* from 1840 to 1844 turned up 629 instances of the name. But none of the Edwins mentioned in those pages had a last name that began with "A," aside from one mention of a ship captain named Edwin J. Ames, who was killed instantly while sailing in the Indian Ocean when a whale's tail slapped him.

38. *Noah Webster's First Edition of an American Dictionary of the English Language*, originally published in 1828 (reprinted in facsimile, Irving on Hudson, NY: Iversen-Norman Associates, 1967), n.p.

39. Edwin A., *A Walk About Vicksburgh, and Other Poems* (Boston, MA: J.V. Pierce, 1844), 42.

40. Dwight E. Robinson, "Fashions in Shaving and Trimming of the Beard: The Men of the *Illustrated London News*, 1842–1972," *American Journal of Sociology* 81, no. 5 (1976): n.p.

41. Advertisements, *Vicksburg Tri-Weekly Sentinel*, April 26, 1844.

42. Edwin A., *Walk About Vicksburgh*, 142.

43. Edwin A., *Walk About Vicksburgh*, 15.

44. Edwin A., *Walk About Vicksburgh*, 54

45. "At a Regular Meeting…," *Sentinel and Expositor for the Country*, January 3, 1843.

46. Rothman, "Hazards of the Flush Times," 651–77.

47. Edwin A., *Walk About Vicksburgh*, 48.

48. Edwin A., *Walk About Vicksburgh*, 49.

49. Edwin A., *Walk About Vicksburgh*, 90–91.

50. Edwin A., *Walk About Vicksburgh*, 30–31.

51. Edwin A., *Walk About Vicksburgh*, 38.

52. Edwin A., *Walk About Vicksburgh*, 160.

53. Edwin A., *Walk About Vicksburgh*, 49

54. Edwin A., *Walk About Vicksburgh*, 48.

55. Edwin A., *Walk About Vicksburgh*, 77

56. Edwin A., *Walk About Vicksburgh*, 42–43; "Mississippi Springs," *Vicksburg Whig*, June 25, 1835.

57. W.C. Webber, *Wild Scenes and Song-Birds* (New York: Leavitt and Allen, 1858), 134.

Chapter 4

58. Elisa De Togni, "The Key in Lincoln's Pocket: Unlocking the Door Union Victory," American Battlefield Trust, https://www.battlefields.org/learn/articles/key-lincolns-pocket.

59. Groom, *Vicksburg*, 272–73, 323–28; Foote, *Beleaguered City*, 154–57.

60. Foote, *Beleaguered City*, 314–15.

61. Foote, *Beleaguered City*, 317.

62. Foote, *Beleaguered City*, 317.

63. Mark Twain, as quoted in Scott Horton, "How Walter Scott Started the American Civil War," *Harper's Magazine*, https://harpers.org/2007/07/how-walter-scott-started-the-american-civil-war/.

64. Stanley B. Burns, "Disease," PBS, https://www.pbs.org/mercy-street/uncover-history/behind-lens/disease/#:~:text=At%20the%20beginning%20of%20the,to%20these%20most%20disabling%20maladies. There is a difference between diarrhea and dysentery, the latter being more serious and accompanied by blood in watery bowel movements. During the Civil War, the two terms were often used interchangeably. Because the particulars of a loose bowel movement were rarely recorded and since the two—diarrhea and dysentery—are so closely related, this chapter also uses the two interchangeably. If this is a mistaken presumption, we beg the medical community's forgiveness—except for those who still rely on nineteenth-century journals of medicine, from whom we assume forgiveness, or at least understanding, is already granted.

65. Robertson, "Dysentery Enemy."

66. Freemon, "Care at the Siege of Vicksburg."

67. Terry L. Jones, "The Best that We Could: How Disease Killed the Civil War Soldiers, Even More Than Guns," *Country Roads*, October 22, 2022, https://countryroadsmagazine.com/art-and-culture/history/disease-in-civil-war-camps/#:~:text=Unsanitary%20living%20conditions%20caused%20dysentery,a%20typical%20Civil%20War%20encampment.

68. John Lustrea, "Eat Your (Desiccated) Vegetables," National Museum of Civil War Medicine, January 3, 2019, https://www.civilwarmed.org/vegetables/.

69. Lustrea, "Eat Your (Desiccated) Vegetables."

70. Brianna Chazin, "How Parasites Changed the American Civil War," National Museum of Civil War Medicine, June 1, 2018, https://www.civilwarmed.org/parasites/.

71. Huffman, Sultana, 110–11.

72. Huffman, Sultana, 42.

73. Rebecca Blackwell Drake, "The Death of General John Bowen," The Battle of Champion Hill, http://battleofchampionhill.org/history/bowen.htm.

74. Drake, "Death of General John Bowen."

Chapter 5

75. History of American Women, "Ann Annis and the Sinking *Sultana*," May 4, 2016, https://www.womenhistoryblog.com/2016/05/ann-annis-and-the-sinking-sultana.html; Huffman, Sultana, 197.

76. The information on Ann Annis's early life and the events leading up to her boarding the *Sultana* can be found at: History of American Women, "Annis and the Sinking *Sultana*"; Find a Grave, "Ann Vessey Annis," https://www.findagrave.com/memorial/38441323/ann-annis.

77. Huffman, Sultana, 178–80.

78. Huffman, Sultana, 179.

79. Huffman, Sultana, 180.

80. Huffman, Sultana, 180–83.

81. The *Sultana* Disaster Museum, "Ann Annis's Statement, May 11, 1865," https://www.sultanadisastermuseum.com/ann-annis.

82. Huffman, Sultana, 185.

83. Huffman, Sultana, 184.

84. Huffman, Sultana, 186–89. The Civil War had destroyed many levees, causing the floodwaters of the Mississippi River to spread miles in both directions.

85. Huffman, Sultana, 208. Alan Huffman writes of one of the *Sultana*'s passengers, a Sister of Charity, on the foredeck "entreating those in the water to avoid drowning one another. Some survivors later said her words did have a calming effect. She would survive in their memories as a totem figure who eventually went up in flames." Captain Cass Mason, who is a large reason the *Sultana* sank, behaved admirably after the explosion. He immediately began tearing anything that could float off the decks and tossing them into the river, all the while urging the panicked passengers to remain calm. Captain Mason was seen on all three decks doing what he could to mitigate the disaster he had launched. He was last seen aboard his ship—a noble end to his ignoble mistake (The *Sultana* Disaster Museum, "Captain James Cass Mason: Unscrupulous Master of the *Sultana*," https://www.sultanadisastermuseum.com/james-mason.)

86. David Szpilman, Joost J.L.M. Bierens, Anthony J. Handley and James P. Orlowski, "Drowning," *The New England Journal of Medicine* 366, no. 22 (October 4, 2012): 2,102–110, https://www.nejm.org/doi/full/10.1056/NEJMra1013317; Huffman, Sultana, 209.

87. Taiwo Victor, "Here's When the Mississippi's Currents Are Most Dangerous," A-Z Animals, August 10, 2022, https://a-z-animals.com/blog/heres-when-the-mississippi-rivers-currents-are-most-dangerous/; Huffman, Sultana, 206–207.

88. Huffman, Sultana, 195.

89. "Commodore" was his first name.

90. Huffman, Sultana, 202–3.

91. The *Sultana* Disaster Museum, "Private Daniel William Lugenbeal," https://www.sultanadisastermuseum.com/william-lugenbeal.

92. Huffman, Sultana, 205.

93. Jon Hamilton, "The Shipwreck That Led Confederate Veterans to Risk All for Union Lives," GBH News, April 28, 2015, https://www.wgbh.org/news/

post/shipwreck-led-confederate-veterans-risk-all-union-lives; Huffman, Sultana, 197–98, 219–22. For an alternate account of Ann's rescue, see Helen E. Chandler's "Ann, aka Anna Vessey Laired Sims Annis and the Sinking of the *Sultana*," Rootsweb.com, https://sites.rootsweb.com/~nwa/aa.html.

94. Huffman, Sultana, 232. Whereas 1,522 passengers died when the *Titanic* sunk, nearly 1,800 died when the *Sultana* went down.

95. Huffman, Sultana, 226.

96. From "In the River Wreck: The *Sultana* Disaster Recalled to Mind," *The Oshkosh* (WI) *Northwestern*, March 30, 1880. This article was found at The *Sultana* Disaster Museum, "Ann Annis: Civilian Passenger," https://www.sultanadisastermuseum.com/ann-annis.

97. Huffman, Sultana, 235.

98. Huffman, Sultana, 274–75. The authors understand there are varying accounts and disagreements regarding the sinking of the *Sultana* and Ann Annis's survival. We have done our best to reconcile opposing viewpoints and, when we could not, use the most likely source or scenario. We believe our story is accurate but acknowledge that we are susceptible to historical error. Perhaps Alan Huffman best sums up the challenges of the historian-storyteller: "Imagine if someone sets out to recreate the interior of your home a century and a half from now, based on a few surviving photos and letters and furniture catalogs from the period; what are the chances that everything would be there and in the right place? The best way to check the facts of a book is against facts in other books, which means, in a sense, that you are sleeping with everyone your sources have slept with, which has obvious disadvantages, but where else are you to turn?"

Chapter 6

99. Present-day Wisconsin.

100. Everett, *Brierfield*, 21–22.

101. Cooper, *Jefferson Davis*, 77.

102. Everett, *Brierfield*, 9. Hurricane Plantation was named after an 1824 storm that destroyed part of house, crippled the plantation owner's brother and plantation caretaker, Isaac, and killed Isaac's infant son.

103. Everett, *Brierfield*, 25.

104. Everett, *Brierfield*, 26–27.

105. Cooper, *Jefferson Davis*, 92.

106. Cooper, *Jefferson Davis*, 92.

107. Cooper, *Jefferson Davis*, 94.

108. Cooper, *Jefferson Davis*, 96–97.

109. Winders, *Panting for Glory*, 37.

110. Winders, *Panting for Glory*, 34–37.

111. Cooper, *Jefferson Davis*, 140.

112. Winders, *Panting for Glory*, 46.

113. Cooper, *Jefferson Davis*, 141.

114. Cooper, *Jefferson Davis*, 143.

115. Cooper, *Jefferson Davis*, 152.

116. Everett, *Brierfield*, 34.

117. Everett, *Brierfield*, 43.

118. Everett, *Brierfield*, 44.

119. Everett, *Brierfield*, 45.

120. Everett, *Brierfield*, 53.

121. Everett, *Brierfield*, 54.

122. Everett, *Brierfield*, 41.

123. Everett, *Brierfield*, 62.

124. Cooper, *Jefferson Davis*, 3.

125. His and Varina's firstborn son died a month before his second birthday.

126. Cooper, *Jefferson Davis*, 325.

127. Cooper, *Jefferson Davis*, 325–27.

128. Cooper, *Jefferson Davis*, 328.

129. Mississippi City is present-day Gulfport and Biloxi.

130. Cooper, *Jefferson Davis*, 651–52.

131. Cooper, *Jefferson Davis*, 652.

132. Cooper, *Jefferson Davis*, 653.

133. Cooper, *Jefferson Davis*, 653–54.

Chapter 7

134. Words by Catherine McAuley (adapted), Elaine Deasy, rsm, music composed by Elaine Deasy rsm (Americas), sung by Marie Cox rsm (The Congregation), "The Suscipe of Catherine McAuley," https://www.mercyworld.org/library/the-suscipe-of-catherine-mcauley/.

135. Sister Mary Paulinus Oakes, RSM, *Angles of Mercy: A Primary Source by Sister Ignatius Sumner of the Civil War and Yellow Fever* (Baltimore, MD: Cathedral Foundation Press, 1998), 11.

136. Oakes, *Angles of Mercy*, x.

137. Oakes, *Angles of Mercy*, xi.

138. Oakes, *Angles of Mercy*, x.

139. Oakes, *Angles of Mercy*, 16.

140. Oakes, *Angles of Mercy*, 17.

141. Oakes, *Angles of Mercy*, 33.

142. Oakes, *Angles of Mercy*, 52.

143. Oakes, *Angles of Mercy*, 20.

144. Oakes, *Angles of Mercy*, 21.

145. Oakes, *Angles of Mercy*, 27–28.

146. Oakes, *Angles of Mercy*, 25.

147. Oakes, *Angles of Mercy*, 53.

148. Oakes, *Angles of Mercy*, 41.

149. Sung by Eddie Redmayne, "Empty Chairs at Empty Tables," lyrics © Universal Music, Careers, Alain Boublil, Music Ltd.

150. Oakes, *Angles of Mercy*, 43.

151. Oakes, *Angles of Mercy*, 42.

152. Oakes, *Angles of Mercy*, 42.

153. Oakes, *Angles of Mercy*, 42.

154. Oakes, *Angles of Mercy*, 60.

155. Oakes, *Angles of Mercy*, 66–67.

156. Oakes, *Angles of Mercy*, 50.

157. Oakes, *Angles of Mercy*, 51.

158. Teilhard de Chardin.

159. The hospital was located thirty miles east of Vicksburg.

160. Oakes, *Angles of Mercy*, 39–40.

161. Oakes, *Angles of Mercy*, 42.

162. Oakes, *Angles of Mercy*, 23.

163. Oakes, *Angles of Mercy*, 46.

164. Louis de Wohl, *Lay Siege to Heaven: A Novel about St. Catherine of Siena* (San Francisco, CA: Ignatius, 1960), 193.

165. Matthew 25:35–40.

166. Oakes, *Angles of Mercy*, 10.

Chapter 8

167. Tom Smith, *The Crescent City Lynchings* (Guilford, CT: The Lyons Press, 2007), XIX–82; "Assassinated," *The Daily Picayune*, October 16, 1890.

168. "It Seems That…," *Lafayette Advertiser*, May 10, 1890; "Telling Testimony," *The New Delta*, July 17, 1890.

169. "Searching Records," *The Daily Picayune*, March 18, 1891.

170. Michael L. Kurtz, "Organized Crime in Louisiana History: Myth and Reality," *Louisiana History* 24, no. 4 (1983): 365–66.

171. Smith, *Crescent City Lynchings*, 83–84.

172. "At the Feet of Clay," *Vicksburg Evening Post*, March 16, 1891.

173. Daniela G. Jager, "The Worst 'White Lynching' in American History: Elites vs. Italians in New Orleans, 1891," *Arbeiten aus Anglistik und Amerikanistik* 27, no. 2 (2002): n.p.

174. "Feet of Clay," *Vicksburg Evening Post*.

175. "The New Orleans Tragedies," *Vicksburg Evening Post*, March 16, 1891.

176. "Vengeance I," *Commercial Herald*, March 15, 1891.

177. "Instantly Killed," *Commercial Herald*, March 24, 1891.

178. "On Habeas Corpus," *Vicksburg Evening Post*, April 3, 1891.

Chapter 9

179. Jordan Rushing, "Prussian Immigrant Establishes Himself in Vicksburg," *Vicksburg Daily News*, January 22, 2023; Vera Ann Fedell, "Vicksburg Facts: The City's Early Italian History," *The Vicksburg Post*, October 21, 2022; *The Lebanese in Mississippi: An Oral History: A Short History of Lebanese Immigration to the State*, https://www.thelebaneseinmississippi.com/about; Maggie Snyder, "Polish Immigrants Became Vicksburg Papermakers," *South County News*, August 16, 2021.

180. Biedenharn, *Heritage*, 20.

181. Biedenharn, *Heritage*, 6–7.

182. Biedenharn, *Heritage*, 7–8.

183. Biedenharn, *Heritage*, 24–25.

184. Biedenharn, *Heritage*, 26, 228. In 1930, Joseph Biedenharn visited his ancestral homeland and saw the original oven his Uncle Henry had learned to cook in. Joseph's daughter, Emmy-Lou, recounted the scene: "On a wall to the right in the same chimney was a Dutch oven made of brick. It was in this oven that Grandfather's brother, Henry, first learned to bake his confections. Father explained, 'My Uncle Henry was not a baker as we know the term; he was an artisan, a conditor, a meister, with his skilled confections, before he came to America.' As Father examined this quaint old oven, his voice quickened with excitement. 'My Uncle Henry built his Dutch oven in the confectionary store in Vicksburg, an exact replica of this one. It was so deep we had a long-handled shovel made to slide the pies and cakes in farther than we could reach. As a boy of fourteen, it was my job to slide the pies.'"

185. Biedenharn, *Heritage*, 30–31.

186. Biedenharn, *Heritage*, 60–61.

187. From a plaque at the Biedenharn Coca-Cola Museum, Vicksburg, MS.

188. From a plaque at the Biedenharn Coca-Cola Museum, Vicksburg, MS.

189. Biedenharn, *Heritage*, 69.

190. Biedenharn, *Heritage*, 71.

191. James Michener, *Iberia* (New York: Fawcett Crest, 1968), 150–51.

192. From a plaque at the Biedenharn Coca-Cola Museum, Vicksburg, MS.

193. Biedenharn, *Heritage*, 62.

Chapter 10

194. The details from this story are drawn from V. Blaine Russel's column, "Vicksburesque," which appeared in the *Vicksburg Evening Post* in the 1930s. Russel's columns appeared daily and offered readers detailed sensory observations about the minutiae of daily life in Vicksburg, along with historical context. Reading Russel's columns as a whole creates a rich and detailed look at Vicksburg in the 1930s ("Vicksburesque," *Vicksburg Evening Post,* July 19, 1930; "Vicksburesque," *Vicksburg Evening Post,* July 26, 1930).

195. "Vicksburesque," *Vicksburg Evening Post,* July 26, 1930.

196. "Vicksburesque," *Vicksburg Evening Post,* August 27, 1930; "Vicksburesque," *Vicksburg Evening Post,* October 7, 1930; "Vicksburesque," *Vicksburg Evening Post,* June 22, 1937.

197. "Vicksburesque," *Vicksburg Evening Post,* January 13, 1931; "Vicksburesque," *Vicksburg Evening Post,* January 28, 1931.

198. "Vicksburesque," *Vicksburg Evening Post,* February 21, 1931.

199. "Vicksburesque," *Vicksburg Evening Post,* August 7, 1931.

200. "Vicksburesque," *Vicksburg Evening Post,* January 28, 1931; "Vicksburesque," *Vicksburg Evening Post,* March 27, 1931.

201. "Vicksburesque," *Vicksburg Evening Post,* September 9, 1930.

202. "Vicksburesqe," *Vicksburg Evening Post,* February 7, 1931.

203. "Vicksburesque," *Vicksburg Evening Post,* December 24, 1931.

204. "Vicksburesque," *Vicksburg Evening Post,* January 17, 1931.

205. "Vicksburesque," *Vicksburg Evening Post,* March 10, 1931.

206. "Vicksburesque," *Vicksburg Evening Post,* September 4, 1930.

207. "Vicksburesque," *Vicksburg Evening Post,* September 17, 1930.

208. "Vicksburesque," *Vicksburg Evening Post,* January 3, 1931; "Vicksburesque," *Vicksburg Evening Post,* February 21, 1931; "Potlikker 'Meet' May Be Called by Huey Long," *Vicksburg Evening Post,* March 2, 1931; "Vicksburesque," *Vicksburg Evening Post,* March 14, 1931.

209. "Vicksburesque," *Vicksburg Evening Post,* October 10, 1930; "Vicksburesque," *Vicksburg Evening Post,* March 3, 1931.

210. "Vicksburesque," *Vicksburg Evening Post,* October 10, 1931.

211. "Vicksburesque," *Vicksburg Evening Post,* September 30, 1931.

212. "Vicksburesque," *Vicksburg Evening Post,* April 2, 1931.

213. "Vicksburesque," *Vicksburg Evening Post,* February 21, 1931.

214. "Vicksburesque," *Vicksburg Evening Post,* January 7, 1931; "Seay's Grill," *Vicksburg Post,* March 14, 1934.

215. "Vicksburesque," *Vicksburg Evening Post,* August 22, 1931.

216. "The Yazoo and Mississippi Valley Railroad and Vicksburg," *Vicksburg Evening Post,* October 13, 1921.

217. "Vicksburesque," *Vicksburg Evening Post*, January 15, 1931.

218. "Vicksburesque," *Vicksburg Evening Post*, July 15, 1930.

Chapter 11

219. Elizabeth Keen, narrative of her experience during the week Rafael McCloud was at large, told in person to Josh Foreman, Starkville, MS, April 18, 2024.

220. Josh Edwards, "Murder Victim Remembered by Colleagues," *Vicksburg Post*, July 2, 2015.

221. Sam Knowlton, "Ex-Coach Pleads Guilty to Having Child Porn," *Vicksburg Post*, May 6, 2006.

222. Josh Edwards, "McCloud Held Without Bond After Hearing," *Vicksburg Post*, July 2, 2015.

223. John Surrat, "Two Vicksburg Men Could Face Charges in Abduction, Death," *Vicksburg Post*, June 30, 2015.

224. Alana Norris, "Downtown Schools, Churches Take Extra Precautions," *Vicksburg Post*, March 3, 2016.

225. John Surratt, "Officers Have One Thought: Get the Bad Guy," *Vicksburg Post*, March 3, 2016.

226. John Surratt, "Kuhn Hospital Becomes Focus of Escapee Hunt," *Vicksburg Post*, March 4, 2016.

227. John Surratt, "Search Goes On," *Vicksburg Post*, March 6, 2016.

228. John Surratt, "Manhunt Over, McCloud Killed," *Vicksburg Post*, March 10, 2016.

Chapter 12

229. Anna Guizerix, "McRaven House Narrowly Spared After 200-Year-Old Oak Falls on Property," *Vicksburg Post*, August 23, 2022, https://www.vicksburgpost.com/2022/08/23/mcraven-house-narrowly-spared-after-200-year-old-oak-falls-on-property/.

230. There is some doubt about whether Andrew Glass ever engaged in banditry. When the McRaven House (known at the time as the Bobb House) was applying for status as an historical landmark, architectural historian Mary McCahon Shoemaker wrote, "The land on which the Bobb House stands was originally part of the extensive holdings of Anthony Glass, an early settler in the area. As the riverport of Vicksburg grew, Glass's holdings near the eastern boundary of the original town were subdivided. William Bobb purchased the 6.3-acre house lot in 1837" (Deed Book J:479). The present authors find no record of Glass's outlawry other than promotional material related to the McRaven House, much of which claims Glass was associated with the

documented and notorious John Murrell. Seth Parker proposes an interesting theory: "Anthony Glass owned the land upon which McRaven currently sits. Around 1836, there was a small residence built by Glass, the Glass Family or an associate. Glass allowed Sheriff Howard to live on the property. When the Sheriff's wife died in 1836, the Sherrif [sic] moved. Due to Sheriff Howard's involvement with the Murrell Excitement, the stories got confused. John Murrell was the real highwayman. Anthony Glass became Andrew Glass. Andrew Glass absorbed the traits of John Murrell. Timelines were woven together. Boom. A legend is born." (Seth Parker, "McRaven/Bobb House, Vicksburg, Mississippi," S. Parker Studios, July 28, 2019, https://sethparker. net/haunted-mcraven-house-vicksburg-mississippi/). Though not certain of its veracity, the present authors have decided to include the Andrew Glass story for three reasons: (1) the original house design suits a highway man's needs; (2) the legend has persisted for centuries and has become a part of Vicksburg lore; and most importantly, (3) the story of Glass the highwayman encapsulates the turn of the nineteenth century Vicksburg with its shifting borders, violence and uncertainty.

231. Sillery, *Haunting of Mississippi*, 20.

232. Stephen Howard, died August 2, 1841; Stephen Howard obituary, *Vicksburg Daily Whig*, August 5, 1841.

233. At the time, it was known as the Bobb House, but for the sake of continuity, "McRaven House" is used here and throughout the chapter. (The National Register of Historic Places also lists the house as the Bobb House.) The current Harrison Street used to be McRaven Street, hence the name.

234. Kate Cummings, *The Journal of a Confederate Nurse*, edited by Richard Barksdale Harwell (Baton Rouge: Louisiana State University Press, 1959), 26. This vignette is taken from the diary of Kate Cumming, a diarist and nurse who served the Confederate army throughout Mississippi, Alabama and Georgia. The quotations are from her time in Corinth, Mississippi, but accurately reflect the challenges of all battlefield nurses and surgeons. The scene outside the McRaven House would have been no different.

235. Cummings, *Journal of a Confederate Nurse*, 25.

236. Cummings, *Journal of a Confederate Nurse*, 25.

237. National Register of Historic Places, "Bobb House—Nomination Form," https://www.apps.mdah.ms.gov/nom/prop/27689.pdf.

238. The story of John Bobb's death can be found in the following two sources: *The Daily Clarion* (Meridian, MS), June 10, 1864, 2; Cotton and Giambrone, *Vicksburg and the War*, 107, 109.

239. Betty Jo Harris, "The Flood of 1927 and the Great Depression: Two Delta Disasters," Folklife in Louisiana: Louisiana's Living Traditions, https://www. louisianafolklife.org/lt/articles_essays/deltadepression.html.

240. Pete Daniel, *Deep'n as It Come: The 1927 Mississippi River Flood* (Fayetteville: University of Arkansas Press, 1996), 45.
241. Find a Grave, "William Murray," https://www.findagrave.com/memorial/209644130/william_murray.
242. Find a Grave, "Ellen Murray," https://www.findagrave.com/memorial/209644216/ellen_murray.
243. Sillery, *Haunting of Mississippi*, 15. If you visit the McRaven House today, you will find, in the words of author Barbara Sillery, "In the front parlor, on the wall nearest the piano, matching four-by-six, sepia-toned photographs capture Annie and Ella as happy, pampered little girls, with long brown curls caught up in large bows, wearing white eyelet dresses."
244. Sillery, *Haunting of Mississippi*, 14.
245. Sillery, *Haunting of Mississippi*, 15.
246. "Nathan Levy, Jr. Has Close Call as Tornado Hits," *Vicksburg Evening Post*, December 7, 1953.
247. "Aftermath of Deadly Tornado Which Struck Vicksburg Saturday," *Vicksburg Post*, December 7, 1953.
248. "28 Killed, 230 Hurt as Twister Shakes City of Vicksburg," *Beckley Post-Herald*, December 7, 1953.
249. Forty-three is not young in his mind. But as the author, he decides which adjectives get used. The "rich and suave" description three paragraphs hence also fall under the purview of "artistic license."

SELECTED BIBLIOGRAPHY

Books

Biedenharn, Emmy Lou. *Biedenharn Heritage*. India: Skilled Books, 1962.

Bunn, Mike. *Fourteenth Colony: The Forgotten Story of the Gulf South During America's Revolutionary Era*. Montgomery, AL: NewSouth Books, 2020.

Chavez, Thomas E. *Spain and the Independence of the United States: An Intrinsic Gift*. Albuquerque: University of New Mexico Press, 2003.

Cooper, William J. *Jefferson Davis, American*. New York: Alfred A. Knopf, 2000.

Cotton, Gordon A., and Jeff Giambrone. *Vicksburg and the War*. Gretna, LA: Pelican, 2004.

Everett, Frank Edgar, Jr. *Brierfield: Plantation Home of Jefferson Davis*. Jackson: University Press of Mississippi, 1971.

Foote, Shelby. *The Beleaguered City: The Vicksburg Campaign*. New York: Modern Library, 1995.

French, Benjamin Franklin, ed. *Historical Collections of Louisiana, Embracing Transactions of Many Rare and Valuable Documents Relating to the Natural, Civil, and Political History of that State*. Vol. 3. New York: Wiley and Putnam, 1851. https://www.loc.gov/resource/rbc0001.2019gen02986v3/?st=gallery.

———. *Historical Collections of Louisiana, Embracing Translations of Many Rare and Valuable Documents Relating to the Natural, Civil and Political History of that State. Compiled with Historical and Biographical Notes*. Vol. 5. New York: Lamport, Blakeman & Law, 1853. https://louisiana-anthology.org/303_download/texts/french--la_historical_docs--vol_5--natchez_massacre/french--historicalcollec05fren.pdf.

Groom, Winston. *Vicksburg, 1863*. New York City: Vintage Books, 2009.

Haynes, Robert V. *The Natchez District and the American Revolution*. Jackson: University Press of Mississippi, 1976.

Huffman, Alan. Sultana*: Surviving the Civil War, Prison, and the Worst Maritime Disaster in American History*. New York City: HarperCollins, 2009.

James, C.L.R. *The Black Jacobins: Toussaint L'Ouverture and the Santo Domingo Revolution*. New York: Vintage Books Edition, 1989.

Myers, Kenneth M. *1729: The True Story of Pierre & Marie Mayeux, the Natchez Massacre and the Settlement of French Louisiana*. Denison, TX: Mayeux Press, 2017.

Penicaut, Andre. *Fleur de Lys and Calumet: Being the Penicaut Narrative of French Adventure in Louisiana*. Translated by Richebourg Gaillard McWilliams. Tuscaloosa: The University of Alabama Press, 1981.

Sillery, Barbara. *The Haunting of Mississippi*. Gretna, LA: Pelican, 2011.

Winders, Richard Bruce. *Panting for Glory: The Mississippi Rifles in the Mexican War*. College Station: Texas A&M University, 2016.

Internet

American Battlefield Trust, www.battlefields.org.

The Battle of Champion Hill, www.battleofchampionhill.org.

Briuer, Frederick L. "The 300th Anniversary of Vicksburg's Fort St. Pierre." MDAH History Is Lunch Talk. January 9, 2019. https://www.youtube.com/watch?v=R23IWG4QEyc.

Country Roads, www.countryroadsmagazine.com.

Encyclopedia of Arkansas, www.encyclopediaofarkansas.net.

Find a Grave, www.findagrave.com.

Freemon, Frank R., MD. "Medical Care at the Siege of Vicksburg, 1863." National Library of Medicine. https://www.ncbi.nlm.nih.gov/pmc/articles/PMC1807986/pdf/bullnyacadmed00010-0027.pdf.

GBH News, www.wgbh.org.

Harper's Magazine, www.harpers.org.

History of American Women, www.womenhistoryblog.com.

Jesuit Online Library, www.jesuitonlinelibrary.bc.edu.

The Lebanese in Mississippi: An Oral History: A Short History of Lebanese Immigration to the State, www.thelebaneseinmississippi.com.

Library of Congress, www.loc.gov.

Mississippi Department of Archives and History, www.mdah.ms.gov.

National Museum of Civil War Medicine, www.civilwarmed.org.

New England Journal of Medicine, www.nejm.org.

PBS, www.pbs.org.

Robertson, Dr. James, Jr. "The Dysentery Enemy." *Radio IQ.* Originally aired on August 22, 1997. www.wvtf.org/civil-war-series/2019-08-30/the-dysentery-enemy.

Rootsweb, www.rootsweb.com.

The *Sultana* Disaster Museum www.sultanadisastermuseum.com.

Vicksburg's Old Court House Museum, www.oldcourthouse.org.

Newspapers

The Daily Clarion (Meridian, MS)

Oshkosh (WI) *Northwestern*

South County News (Vicksburg, MS)

About the Authors

Ryan Starrett was born and raised in Jackson, Mississippi. After receiving degrees from the University of Dallas, Adams State University and Spring Hill College, as well as spending a ten-year hiatus in Texas, he returned home to continue his teaching career at his alma mater St. Joseph Catholic School. He lives in Madison with his wife, Jackie, and two children, Joseph Padraic and Penelope Rose O.

Josh Foreman was born and raised in the Jackson metro area. He is a sixth-generation Mississippian and an eleventh-generation Southerner. He lived, taught and wrote in South Korea from 2005 to 2014. He holds degrees from Mississippi State University and the University of New Hampshire. He lives in Starkville, Mississippi, with his wife, Melissa, and his three children, Keeland, Genevieve and Ulrich.